Fill My Cup, Lord . . .

A Teatime Devotional

Emilie Barnes

with Anne Christian Buchanan

Cover by Garborg Design Works, Minneapolis, Minnesota

FILL MY CUP, LORD

Copyright © 1996 by Harvest House Publishers
Eugene, Oregon 97402

Cover art by Sandy Lynam Clough
The cover art in this book is copyrighted by Sandy Lynam Clough and may not be reproduced without permission.

Library of Congress Cataloging-in-Publication Data
Barnes, Emilie.
  Fill my cup, Lord / Emilie Barnes with Anne Christian Buchanan.
     p. cm.
    ISBN 1-56507-358-4 (hardcover)
    ISBN 0-7369-0630-4 (trade)
   1. Bible. O.T. Psalms XXIII—Meditations. 2. Christian life—Meditations.
   I. Title.
BS1450 23rd.B37   1996
242—dc20   95-46904
                             CIP

Printed in the United States of America.

01 02 03 04 05 06 / BP / 8 7 6 5 4 3 2 1

To my daughter, Jenny, our Princess #1
Without you, my sweet one,
this book would have never been written.
I love you deeply and dearly.

Contents

A Word for Thirsty Souls

The Lord is my shepherd; I shall not want.

Psalm 23:1

H ow can so many people's lives be so full and their hearts and souls be so thirsty?

That's what I find myself wondering as the years go racing by me.

At church, at our seminars, even in restaurants or airports I meet men and women whose schedules are packed, who are pouring all their energy into keeping up with their lives and soon find themselves all poured out. Physically and emotionally and spiritually, they are desperately in need of a refill.

And of course, I run on empty, too, at times. My tasks as a writer and speaker, as a wife and mother and grandmother and friend, pull at me until I feel parched and drained.

That's when I find special meaning in that wonderful old song I heard for the first time so many years ago as a young Jewish girl who had recently come to know the Lord.

"Fill my cup, Lord," the singer sang that evening. That was long before I began my collection of lovely china teacups. It was before my children came, before my mother died, before my writing and speaking ministry was even a gleam of possibility. And yet something deep in my spirit echoed the cry of that song.

Today, knowing a lot more about teacups and even more about the ways that life can drain us, I find that "Fill my cup" is a constant cry of my thirsty heart.

Sometimes, during especially trying times, I feel like Oliver Twist standing there with his tiny, polished bowl, pleading with hungry eyes, "Please, Sir, I want some more."

Those are times when I am at the end of my rope, when I know I have no means of nourishing myself and am willing to risk humiliation to beg for the life I need. At those times my gracious Lord Jesus, so unlike the selfish beadle in Dickens' story, pours out his presence with an especially generous hand.

More often, though, I find myself holding up a cup that is not quite empty, a heart not quite that humble and hungry. Sometimes my cup holds the old, cold residues of rancid ideas or moldy attitudes or leftover values and stubborn pain. I still need the Lord to fill my cup, but first I need to have it emptied and rinsed clean. That requires both my willingness and the Lord's grace.

Something else about the cup I hold up for the Lord's filling: it's cracked and flawed, the gleam of the porcelain marred with imperfections. I need to remember that no matter what my polish or glaze, I am still an earthen vessel. And sometimes I feel as patched and glued as the one cup I was able to rescue after a shelf in my armoire came crashing down. Perhaps that's why I seem to empty out so easily. I leak, so I need refilling on a daily or even an hourly basis.

"Fill my cup, Lord."

I hope that's your heartcry, too, as you open this book.

I imagine you sitting there quietly, perhaps with a cup of fragrant tea at your elbow and this book in your lap. Perhaps you have managed to carve out a tiny minute of respite from ringing phones and crying children. Or perhaps your days are lonely and too long, and you've taken this minute as a way of structuring the empty hours.

Whatever your circumstances, you, too, can hold up your cup and it will be filled.

If your cup is polished and dry, hold it out for the Lord's plentiful pouring.

If your cup is full of the old and the unsatisfying, hold it up for the Lord's cleansing.

If your cup is cracked and broken, hold it up anyway, for the Lord's resources are plentiful and can keep even leaky cups replenished.

Come to him as you are, cup in hand, and hold it up to receive his blessings.

And then you will say, as I have said over and over again in wonder and amazement—

"Surely . . . my cup runneth over."

Fill my cup, Lord . . .

I offer you my cup of stress

that you may fill it

with quietness.

I

A Cup of Quietness

He makes me to lie down in green pastures;
He leads me beside the still waters.
Psalm 23:2

uiet time.

It's a lovely phrase, isn't it? To me, "quiet time" summons up images of stillness and serenity, of a quiet communion with God on a beautiful garden patio or a cozy window seat—reading his Word and praying and journaling while a fragrant cup of tea steams at my elbow.

And I have had wonderful quiet times like that.

But these days, I have to confess, my quiet times are not always so quiet—at least not at first. Sometimes they start out more like silent wrestling matches as I struggle with my fears, my worries, my pain.

Do you have times like that? Times when you seek out solitude, flee into stillness, only to find that your worries have followed and refuse to leave you alone? Or times when your schedule is so demanding that quiet time with God feels like just one more chore you can't manage?

If so, I have good news for you.

A quiet spirit is not a requirement for a quiet time with the Lord.

Yes, I need to be willing to come to him, to offer him my cup filled with whatever is troubling me. But if I do that, I have found that he can supply the quiet spirit. If I can manage to hand over that cup of trouble, he can and will fill it to overflowing with serenity and peace.

What a wonderful thing to know, to remember, to remind yourself of when you feel overwhelmed with busyness or with pain. You don't have to come to him quiet. You just need to come to him.

The last few years have not been easy ones for our family. Not only has our schedule been packed with important but wearying obligations, but the trauma of an impending divorce has also torn a big rip in the fabric of our lives. I've had to watch as people I love make decisions I don't understand or approve of, and I've agonized as others I love suffer hurts I can't soothe. I've had to wait for answers and understanding and resolution that just haven't come yet.

That's why so many of my quiet times lately have started out anything but quiet. Often I have been angry or torn or worried or scared.

But that's why I need the quiet in the first place. When my mind is full of clamor and my cup is full of trouble, that's when I most need to hear God's still small voice, and to feel his peace.

This is what I'm learning once again as I hold up my cup to the Lord and seek to spend time with him:

My quiet time is not a gift I give to God.

My quiet time is a gift God gives to me.

I don't offer him my quiet time. I simply offer him my time, my self. He's the one who provides the quiet spirit.

I come to him with my cup of confusion and worry. He's the one who takes that cup and empties it and then pours it full of quietness and peace.

He supplies the quiet. I supply the time.

That's one reason I can have quiet time, if necessary, in places that are not absolutely quiet. Quiet doesn't always require solitude. In fact, I've had some of my most meaningful quiet times on airplanes or in crowded restaurants, with engine noise buffeting my ears and people pressed in around me. My spirit was with the Lord, silently holding up my cup to him, and he provided the gift of quietness in the midst of a whirlwind.

But quietness does seem to require that I make the conscious effort to get away from the distractions of those who need me or who claim my attention. That's why I can have quiet time on a noisy airplane where no one knows me but not during a family dinner or on the floor of a conference where I am speaking. I need to pull away, to shut a door, to put space between me and the ordinary demands of my day. And in order for that to happen, I usually need to schedule my time for being with God.

But I don't need to "get quiet" in order to draw near to God. I just need to be willing to come to him.

Of course, it's wonderful to go to a place where physical quietness can help foster spiritual quietness. God has always spoken quieting words to me through his creation, so I love to have my quiet times out of doors. I love to go to a park, into a yard, under a tree—where I can see the butterfly flap its wings in spring or watch the colored leaves drift off the trees in fall. God works in my heart through nature, soothing my spirit with growing things and gentle breezes.

For several years now, my quiet times have tended to coincide with my morning walks. Yes, I love a quiet moment with a cup of tea, but I prefer company for tea. And yes, I have my daily times with my prayer notebook, when I try to be faithful to my prayer promises, interceding for my family and for my church and for those who have requested my prayers.

But when my cup is full of trouble and I really need to be alone with God, I like to lace up my tennies and set out on the path along the long irrigation canal that runs through our town.

I know that two-mile course now like the back of my hand. I know where the rocks jut up, where the path grows narrow, where the orange blossoms smell the sweetest, where a recent rain will make a mud puddle on the path. I feel safe among the many other joggers and walkers (and their dogs) that use the path. And somehow the rhythm of my Reeboks on that familiar path helps me walk my thoughts toward my heavenly Father.

Because I know the route so well, I sometimes read as I walk—or read a bit and then walk a bit. I carry a little book of scriptural prayers, and I read a few and then let them work into my mind as I stride along. Over the past year or so, I've prayed through several of these books more than once (I write the date in the back cover when I finish one and start over).

But I don't wait until I feel spiritual to start walking. I simply put one foot in front of the other. As I walk I simply let my thoughts and feelings and confusions and stresses rise up in my mind, turning them over to God. And most of the time, by the time my forty-five-minute walk is over, the quiet has usually come.

Sometimes it takes awhile. Most days, in fact, it takes at least twenty minutes for the noise and busyness of my everyday life to sift out of my head and for my internal strife to settle down. It seems to take that twenty minutes of walking to get my cup rinsed out and ready for the Lord's filling.

I may not be consciously praying or even thinking during that time. I'm simply walking and letting the breeze wash over me and listening to the birds sing and smelling the orange blossoms and letting the Scriptures or whatever else I've been reading speak to my spirit in the silence.

And then, in the last twenty minutes of my walk, something almost always happens. The "to dos" and "I've gottas" and "but what abouts" in my head begin to subside, and God's peace begins to settle into my spirit. And then, when I'm finally able to listen, God whispers his word of peace and comfort, or guidance and challenge.

Sometimes I remember a passage of Scripture. Sometimes a knotty problem seems to unravel itself in my head. Sometimes I am simply strengthened to go on with my life. Tears often flow—tears of relief and release as my cup of troubles is poured out and the quietness flows in to take its place.

No, it doesn't always take that long. I have found that if I offer to God whatever time I have, he honors that time. If I only have fifteen minutes but bring those fifteen minutes to him, he can give me what I need in those fifteen minutes. But, then the sweet taste of his peace leaves me wanting more and more.

And no, it doesn't happen every single time. It's not a cut-and-dried transaction: I come to God; he gives me peace. It's a relationship. The peace comes from spending time with the one who speaks in silence. The quietness comes from being with him and letting him rearrange my thought processes.

There have been a few times on the canal path (and on the patio and on the airplane) when nothing seems to change—when I have come to God agitated and gone away agitated. Sometimes in retrospect I can understand what happened. I was holding on too tightly to my troubles, unwilling to give up control even to God. Or I needed to learn something or do some growing, and God was using my discomfort to motivate me. I don't know all the answers for those times when my quiet time never got quiet. God rarely works on my schedule, and sometimes my cup filled with peace more slowly than I expected.

But I have to tell you that those times have been rare, even in the difficult years. Almost always, I have come away from my quiet times with my cup over-flowing. Again and again, when I gave the Lord my chaos, he has given me his peace.

More and more, that is what I am yearning to do.

The longer I live, the more I thirst for those quiet times in my heavenly Father's presence, the more I long to climb up into the lap of my Abba-Daddy and enjoy the security of those everlasting arms. Sometimes I feel like a toddler stretching my own arms up, dancing on my toes, begging to be held by the One who loves me so much.

"Up, Daddy. Want up."

And then he lifts me up.

The longer I live, the more I know that if I will just hold up my cup to him, even my cup of anger and stress and trouble and confusion, he will be faithful to fill my cup with the peace of his presence.

Savoring God's Word . . .
A Sip of Quietness

When He gives quietness, who then can make trouble?

Job 34:29

I wait for the Lord, my soul waits,
And in His word I do hope.

Psalm 130:5

My soul, wait silently for God alone,
For my expectation is from Him.

Psalm 62:5

Better is a handful with quietness
Than both hands full, together with toil
and grasping for the wind.

Ecclesiastes 4:6

In returning and rest you shall be saved;
in quietness and confidence shall be your strength.

Isaiah 30:15

Peace I leave with you, My peace I give to you; not as
the world gives do I give to you. Let not your heart be
troubled, neither let it be afraid.

John 14:27

For God is not the author of confusion but of peace.

1 Corinthians 14:33

Be anxious for nothing, but in everything by prayer and supplication, with thanksgiving, let your requests be made known to God; and the peace of God, which surpasses all understanding, will guard your hearts and minds through Christ Jesus.

Philippians 4:6,7

Come to Me, all you who labor and are heavy laden, and I will give you rest. Take My yoke upon you and learn from Me, for I am gentle and lowly in heart, and you will find rest for your souls. For My yoke is easy and My burden is light.

Matthew 11:28

Now to Him who is able to do exceedingly abundantly above all that we ask or think, according to the power that works in us, to Him be glory.

Ephesians 3:20,21

Fill my cup, Lord . . .

I offer you my cup of criticism

that you may fill it

with encouragement.

2

A Cup of Encouragement

He restores my soul.
Psalm 23:3

"*W*hat a beautiful reception," I thought as I
flipped through the recently developed stack of
photographs.

There was my newly married niece, her face
flushed with happiness. There was her new husband,
beaming and proud. There were the children, dressed
up and excited, and the older ladies beaming with sat-
isfaction at another wedding in the family.

And there I was in my white Battenburg lace
dress—looking pretty good, if I did say so myself!

I should have looked good. I had poured a lot of
effort into pulling myself together perfectly for the
occasion, paying special attention to my hair, my hose,

my shoes, my bag. Trying so hard to get everything just exactly right so that my elderly auntie, for once, would have nothing to criticize.

Well, I finally did it, I thought as I flipped another picture. There was my aunt sitting at her table with a big smile on her face. My smile was big, too, as I remembered it. For the first time in my memory, she hadn't said a single critical word about how I was dressed or how my makeup looked or anything else. I'd talked to her on the phone several times since then, and she still hadn't made a negative comment.

I glanced at the clock. I really needed to call her again. She was very independent, even in her eighties, but I still tried to check on her every day or two.

Auntie was in a wonderful mood when she answered the phone. She had gotten her pictures, too. So we reminisced about the ceremony, speculated on how the new couple would get along, and replayed the events of the reception.

"And, oh, Emilie," she enthused, "you looked just beautiful."

By now I was actually grinning. This was almost too good to be true.

And then she added in a thoughtful voice, "Emilie . . . you really need to consider getting a padded bra."

Zing. I could feel my grin slipping down to the floor, that old familiar knot tightening my stomach.

I should have seen it coming, of course. It was only the hundred-millionth time she had done that to me. (I was beginning to realize that she did it with everyone she loved.) But that didn't keep the words from stinging—as they always stung. With one little remark, my auntie had managed once more to fill my cup with criticism.

Do you know somebody like that, who seems to delight in pouring doses of criticism? If you don't, just wait a little bit, and one will almost certainly come knocking at your door. Your critic may even be ringing your doorbell or calling you on the phone right now. Someone you just can't please. Someone who excels in bowling over your confidence with just a word or a look.

It may be direct, overt, controlling:

"You shouldn't pick up the baby when he cries."

"I'm afraid blue just isn't your color."

"Thank you, but it's just not our style. I know you won't mind if I return it."

Or it may be more subtle—a backhanded compliment or just a calculating sniff and a martyred look:

"You're so patient. If my children acted like that I'd be mortified."

"Well, yes, I suppose so . . ."

But no matter how the criticism is poured, the message is clear. You did it wrong. Your efforts just don't measure up. You just aren't good enough . . . smart enough . . . pretty enough.

It's so hard to live freely and creatively and lovingly with that kind of criticism. It's hard to risk flying high when you're always afraid of being shot down. I know, because my critical auntie had been pouring out caustic cupfuls for me ever since I could remember.

It wasn't that she didn't care about me. In fact, she had always made it clear that I was special to her. But my auntie's critical spirit led her to express her love with constant attempts to control and change me. From the time I was small, nothing about me had ever been quite right for her—my hair, my speech, my manners, my clothes, my children, or anything else.

And how did I respond?

For years, I just tried harder.

I spent so much of my life in a constant struggle to live up to my aunt's impossible standards.

I would visit the hairdresser and have my nails done before a visit. She would give me the number of *her* hairdresser and manicurist.

I would scour the stores for just the right birthday gift. She would return it.

I would choose my words and my grammar with care, trying so hard not to say anything wrong. She would still find something to criticize.

And then it finally hit me.

All my life I had been holding out my cup to my auntie, waiting for her to fill it with encouragement and praise. And she couldn't do it! Her own cup was too full of a critical spirit to pour anything different into mine. Holding up a bigger or better or more beautiful cup wasn't going to make any difference. And Satan was still using her poured-out criticism to make me feel inadequate and insecure and thus damage my ability to share Christ's love.

If I wanted my cup to hold anything other than criticism, I needed to stop holding it out to my auntie so trustingly. When she poured the criticism in anyway— as she was bound to do—I needed to take what I could learn from her critical words and then dump the bitter brew down the drain.

But it wasn't enough just to empty my cup. If I did, my aunt or someone else would fill it up again. What I needed to do was to keep my cup filled with love and acceptance and affirmation and encourage- ment from a dependable Source. I had to decide who I wanted to listen to—who was going to have power over me. And making that decision is what would enable me to empty out the criticism, wash out the cup, and then get it refilled from God's bubbling bounty of encouragement.

That, gradually, was what I learned to do. But it didn't happen all at once. It took a lot of time and practice and prayer. That particular painful afternoon, God and I had already been working on this process of emptying and filling for several years.

What did I do in response to her criticism?

I thanked my aunt for the idea. (I hadn't worn a padded bra since high school.) Then I pictured myself slowly turning over that cup of criticism and pouring it out, wiping it clean, holding it up again. And I prayed, *Please, Lord, fill my cup with your love. Let me respond to her criticism with gentleness. Even though she fills my cup with criticism, let me fill her cup with encouragement.*

And, please, Lord, I added, *don't ever let me act like that to others. Teach me to see and express only what is good and healthy in my friends and family.*

How often, I wonder, have I filled others' cups with my criticism by stressing the negative and not focusing on the positive? Whether I liked it or not, I was trained by an expert to look at others with a critical eye. And when your cup is full of criticism, it's so easy to let it overflow into the cups of those around you! That's another reason it's so important that I keep emptying the cup of criticism and filling it with positive things—so I can fill others' cups with encouragement instead of criticism.

First Peter 3:4 reminds us of the importance of cultivating the "inner self, the unfading beauty of a gentle and quiet spirit, which is of great worth in God's sight" (NIV). That's what I want for my life—a cup of encouragement and affirmation rather than a cup of criticism.

Yet even as I write this, I realize I may have fallen into being critical toward my critical aunt! Yes, she had her faults. But I truly believe she did the best she could with what she was given. And she had so many good qualities. She gave generously to those in need and to many who were not in need. She modeled hard work, rigorous honesty, and the nurturing of family connections. (Until she died, she regularly sent money to our extended family in Romania.) She left me so much—not only her material possessions, but also a heritage of helping others. As I empty my cup of criticism, I want to fill it with encouragement and affirmation and also with gratitude for this woman who loved me and shaped me.

There is so much about any person that is good and beautiful. So focusing on the positive doesn't mean being naive or unrealistic or blind. It simply means learning to accept myself and others for what we are—human beings with faults and good points and also the capacity to grow.

It also means I'm learning to accept the fact that I'm not the one in charge of the universe. It's not my job to change everybody or even to enlighten the world about its problems! Besides, criticism hardly ever changes anybody—except to make the criticized person more angry, resentful, stubborn, and, perhaps, critical of others.

Now, I am not saying we should never speak with one another about problems. I am not saying we should blind ourselves to faults or ignore difficulties. I am not saying we should always sit on our opinions and bite our tongues. And I am certainly not saying we should never return gifts or give our honest opinion about how someone's hair looks.

There is a difference between honest discussion and hurtful accusation. There is a difference between being aware of someone's faults and shattering that person's confidence. There is a big difference between tactfully returning a gift or stating an opinion and filling someone's cup with criticism.

But discerning that difference may involve some honest self-evaluation. A critical spirit can be easy to rationalize, especially in the name of honesty or help-fulness. When there's doubt, I truly believe it's better not to say anything.

So, is your cup filled with criticism?

Are you holding onto your cup and filling the cups of others with the bitter brew?

If you think that's possible, I urge you to stop and pour out your cup of criticism before it poisons you and the people you love. Then begin the work of cleaning out the hurts in your life that make you critical of others.

When criticism starts to fill your cup again, and it will, recognize it for what it is and stop letting it in. Instead, make a point of pouring beauty and love into your cup and the cups of others. Look for something to admire in yourself and others and make a point of expressing that admiration.

If that's hard, think again. We are all children of God, created by him. He made us each beautiful in his sight. Make the effort to find that beauty in yourself and others.

I'm not saying it's easy—the habit of criticism can be deeply ingrained. My auntie remained critical of me until the day she died, and I'm sure I have moments when the old poisonous brew drips from my cup into someone else's.

But the cycle of criticism really can be broken. This is how it works:

First, you examine your cup. You take a tiny sip to see if there's something there you need—some truth you need to hear, even in that unpleasant form. Then you turn your cup, dump out that poisonous draft, and hold out your cup to be filled with God's love and acceptance and encouragement.

And you do it again, repeating the process whenever the criticism begins to flow. Better yet, you keep your cup so full of good things that there's no room for the biting, critical words.

You can do that, you know, because the Lord is always there for you, waiting to fill your cup with encouragement and affirmation, waiting mercifully to restore your soul when it has been shriveled by criticism. He does it through the words of Scripture, through the soft whisper of his Holy Spirit, and especially through the people who love and accept and support you.

Surely I wouldn't have been able to cope with my auntie's criticism if there hadn't been people who kept my cup brimming with encouragement and affirmation. But God has filled my cup generously through these special people in my life.

I think of my mother, who always believed in me and excelled at the gentle art of teaching without criticizing.

Or I think of my husband, Bob, whose ongoing affirmation has lifted me higher than I ever imagined, and my children and grandchildren, who encourage me in a hundred ways.

Mentors such as Florence Littauer lovingly badgered me into becoming a speaker and a writer when I had no idea I had anything to say or any gift for saying it.

My special friends, who know me so well and love me anyway, give me daily encouragement to keep on.

And I am profoundly grateful to all the hundreds of women who read my books and attend my seminars and then call or write to let me know that God has touched their lives through me.

If God, who knows me more intimately than even Bob or my mother, can use me as a channel of his blessings—and make no mistake, he uses you, too!—then how can I let my cup remain full of criticism? How can I not be encouraged when I remember that God has not only accepted me, but wants to use me to do his work in the world?

That is not to say that everything about me is acceptable to God! In fact, the Scriptures make it clear that I am always falling short of the mark. I never get it all right, no matter how hard I try. No one does.

But here's the amazing lesson for those of us whose cup of criticism has too often been full.

God himself, when confronted with the enormity of human sin, didn't respond by criticizing us. He didn't sit up there in heaven and harp about the way we humans manage to mess up every good thing he ever made.

What he did was become a human being and live among us.

And there's more.

Of all the people on earth, there has been only One with the right and the power to criticize any other human. There has only been One without sin, one person worthy to throw stones at others. And he didn't do it.

What he did was die for us. And that fact alone is enough to fill my cup to overflowing.

But there's more to the story about my critical auntie.

Less than three years after my niece's wedding reception, this same aunt lay dying in her hospital bed. She was eighty-eight. She had fought death to the end with the same determination she had brought to the rest of her life. But now she was very tired, and we knew the end was near.

I remember the last evening in particular. Darkness had already fallen by the time I arrived at the hospital, and the soft lighting in my auntie's room contrasted with the harsh lights of the corridor.

"Your auntie has been very peaceful today," the woman in the next bed told me in her soft Jamaican accent. She was a very sick woman herself, going blind with diabetes. We had gotten to know her a little during the past few days.

I looked at my auntie. Maybe she did look peaceful, compared to her hard days of fighting. But she was so clammy and thin and the color had gone from her and her breathing was so heavy. And as I sat there beside her I began to think back over the years, about the time she had spent with me and the gifts she had given me and also about all the pain she had brought to my life. Somehow it all seemed minor now.

So I put my arms around my auntie, and I put my hankie to her brow, and I began to recite the Twenty-third Psalm, "The Lord is my shepherd, I shall not want. . . ."

And then the soft voice from the next bed was joining in, reciting with me. "He maketh me to lie down in green pastures; he leadeth me beside the still waters. He restoreth my soul. . . ."

In the silence of the bare room that sweet Jamaican woman and I recited the familiar words of the psalm. We finished, and then we recited it again, and it was as if angels were hovering in the room.

And now, I thought, my aunt really did look peaceful—or perhaps the peace was in my heart. I pulled the covers up and I tucked her in, and I left. That was the last time I was able to look into my auntie's face, her eyes, and hold her hand, because she died a very few moments after that.

I later found out that the woman in the next bed, a brilliant woman who spoke five languages, had learned the Twenty-third Psalm as a little girl and recited it every night before she went to sleep. What a blessing she was to me in those difficult hours. How she filled my cup with encouragement!

I truly do not know where my auntie is now. Unlike my mother, who came to know Jesus in her later years, my Jewish auntie died without acknowledging the Messiah.

But I do know that the last words she heard were God's Word, and her last human contact was a loving embrace. And I know that happened only because I, by God's grace, had learned to empty out my cup of criticism. God's great and amazing mercy to me during that difficult time was the gift of powerful acceptance and prayer for this woman who had hurt me so deeply, but who also loved me much. And, oh, how that beautiful gift helped to restore my soul.

Savoring God's Word . . .
A Sip of Encouragement

Do not withhold good from those to whom it is due,
when it is in the power of your hand to do so.

Proverbs 3:27

There were some who were indignant among themselves,
and said, "Why was this fragrant oil wasted? For it might
have been sold for more than three hundred denarii and
given to the poor." And they criticized her sharply. But
Jesus said, "Let her alone. Why do you trouble her? She has
done a good work for Me."

Mark 14:4-6

Judge not, and you shall not be judged. Condemn not,
and you shall not be condemned. Forgive, and you will be
forgiven.

Luke 6:37

For God did not send His Son into the world to condemn
the world, but that the world through Him might be
saved.

John 3:17

There is therefore now no condemnation to those who are in Christ Jesus, who do not walk according to the flesh, but according to the Spirit.

Romans 8:1

Whatever things are true, whatever things are noble, whatever things are just, whatever things are pure, whatever things are lovely, whatever things are of good report, if there is any virtue and if there is anything praiseworthy —meditate on these things.

Philippians 4:8

Encourage the timid, help the weak, be patient with everyone. Make sure that nobody pays back wrong for wrong, but always try to be kind to each other and to everyone else.

1 Thessalonians 5:14,15 (NIV)

Do not speak evil of one another. . . . He who speaks evil of a brother and judges his brother, speaks evil of the law and judges the law. But if you judge the law, you are not a doer of the law but a judge.

James 4:11

And above all things have fervent love for one another, for "love will cover a multitude of sins."

1 Peter 4:8

Fill my cup, Lord . . .

I offer you my cup of resentment

that you may fill it

with forgiveness.

3

A Cup of Forgiveness

*He leads me in the paths of
righteousness for His name's sake.*
Psalm 23:3

$\mathcal{I}$t was an unbelievably beautiful morning in the
spring. A golden sun was climbing in a brilliant blue,
cloudless sky, and the sunlight sparkled in the cool air.
Bob and I had decided to have our breakfast out on
the patio, where fountain was dancing containers of
pansies and mums.

Smiling at each other, we drank our orange juice
and enjoyed the quiet beginning of a perfect day. Little
curls of steam rose from our freshly buttered muffins
as Bob read a page from a devotional for husbands
and wives. We each enjoyed a cantaloupe half as we
chatted about the grandchildren and the garden. Then,
as we lingered over our fragrant cups of coffee, Bob
pulled out our jar of Mom's Canned Questions.

A friend of ours developed this wonderful little product, which we sell at our More Hours in My Day seminars. It's really just a decorated jar full of little slips of paper, but each slip contains a question designed to stimulate thought and discussion. We use it often when we have company and when we are by ourselves, and the questions have brought us both tears and laughter as they helped us know each other better.

As usual, Bob drew out a question and passed the jar to me. I reached in and pulled out a slip. And then I seemed to feel dark clouds rolling in to block the sunshine as I read my question. My impulse was to say "Forget it" and stuff that little slip of paper back in the jar.

What was on the paper?

Just this: "What would you do if you could spend one day with your dad?"

Such a simple question. But the memories it evoked had the power to fill my cup with pain and anger and resentment.

You see, my dad was a brilliant man, a creative Viennese chef. He used to get standing ovations for the food he prepared. From what I'm told, he doted on me as a little child, and I've inherited some of his creativity in the kitchen.

And yet my dad was also a raging alcoholic. Living in our home meant always living on edge, never knowing when he might explode. One wrong word from any of us, and the spaghetti sauce would be dumped down the toilet or down the sink; the pots and pans would be whipped off the stove and the plates off the table. There would be shouting; there would be arguments. And although my father never physically abused me, he did take his rage out on my mother and brother.

In response to my father's rage, I almost gave up talking. If saying the wrong thing could trigger an explosion, I reasoned perhaps it was better not to say anything at all. So I became intensely introverted and fearful, and I wished my father dead many times. When I was eleven, he really did die, leaving a cloud of guilt and resentment that hung over my life long after I thought I had forgotten.

Even after my dad died, I still didn't talk much. When I met Bob and we began dating, he used to say to me, "Emilie, you've got to talk." And then so many wonderful things began to happen in my life. The most important was that Bob introduced me to Jesus, and I became a Christian. Then Bob asked me to marry him, and my Jewish mama (who was very wise) surprised me by giving her consent. Relatives criticized her for letting her precious seventeen-year-old marry a Gentile, but my mama sensed that Bob could give me the love and stability I needed.

45

Mama was right. After Bob and I were married and I felt secure for the first time in my life, I began to talk. Now I even talk for a living—and there are probably times when Bob wishes I would stop talking!

Our lives went on. Little Jenny was born, then Brad, and I threw my energy into raising our children and making a home for us all. Bob worked as an educator, then a businessman. The kids grew up and left home. Through an amazing series of events, More Hours in My Day became a book, then an exciting ministry. My mother came to know the Messiah and moved in with us. Grandbabies were born.

Through it all, I didn't think all that much about my dad. He was in my past, which I had put behind me. I was a Christian, and I knew I was supposed to forgive others. I read in the Bible that we had to forgive if God were going to forgive us. So yes, I forgave my dad—or so I thought.

And then one day Florence Littauer invited me to go to a seminar that her friend Lana Bateman was conducting at a nearby hotel. I didn't really know what it was about, only that Florence thought it would be good for anyone. So I just walked into that hotel room . . . and almost immediately the tears began to flow.

The spirit of God had prepared my heart for a remarkable experience in coming to terms with my past and growing closer to him. Part of what I realized that weekend was that I still had a lot of pain concerning my father. I thought I had forgiven him when I had really only boxed up my anger and resentment and stored it away—like sealing a bunch of toxic waste in a barrel and burying it underground. In order truly to forgive, I had to bring out that anger and resentment and actually hand them over to God, trusting him to take them away from me.

That weekend I began the process of truly forgiving my father and letting God restore my relationship with him. I admitted to myself that I needed healing. Even though my dad was long dead, I wrote him a long letter, pouring out both my love and my fury. I confessed the anger and bitterness I had held onto for so long without even knowing it was there.

All this was hard work. It demanded all my courage, all my energy. But what a difference that weekend made in my life. I poured out my cup of resentment. I let the Lord wash it bright and clean, and then I knew the awestruck wonder of having my cup filled to the brim with sparkling forgiveness—forgiveness for my father, and forgiveness for myself. What a wonderful feeling! I was clean, washed clean, drinking from a clean cup.

But that was not the end of the story.

Not long afterward, someone mentioned my father. And I was shocked to recognize the quick flash of anger, the stubborn, involuntary clenching of my jaw. The resentment was still there, or it had come back.

What was going on? Was that whole difficult weekend in vain?

Hadn't I emptied my cup of bitterness and let God fill it with forgiveness?

Oh yes!

The forgiveness I experienced that weekend was real. But now I was learning something very important about my cup of forgiveness.

It leaks!

For most of us, most of the time, forgiveness is an ongoing process, not a "done deal." Forgiveness is an absolute necessity for healthy living, the only known antidote to the bitterness and resentment and anger that flow naturally and abundantly when selfish human beings rub up against other selfish human beings.

But my cup of forgiveness seems to be one of the leakiest cups I own. It can be brimming over one day and empty the next—or refilled with bitter resentment over the very same hurt I thought I had forgiven. In fact, I can quickly accumulate enough pain and hurt and resentment to fill several cups, stacked up and precariously balanced.

All this can be discouraging.

"God, I thought I had let go of that!"

"God, I really want to forgive. Why is it so hard?"

But it can also be a source of faith, a reminder that we must keep going back to our forgiving Father for this cleansing elixir. We can't manufacture it ourselves; it always comes by the grace of God.

I love King David's beautiful song of forgiveness, Psalm 51. David's life was filled with one sin after another—things that were done to him and things that he did to others. But he knew the secret of coming to God for forgiveness. "Create in me a clean heart, O God," he prayed. He asked God not only to forgive, but to "wash me . . . whiter than snow."

How beautiful our cup can be when we offer it to the Lord—washed and cleaned, white and pure as the fresh-fallen snow, filled to the brim with beautiful, sparkling forgiveness. Why would we ever want to hold on to our scummy resentment when we could drink from that shining cup?

A friend of mine recently shared with me a great picture of how God's forgiveness works.

This friend works as a parent-aide in her daughter's third-grade class, and on one particular day she was assisting in an art lesson—a watercolor class. Each eight-year-old was given a piece of paper, a box of watercolors, a brush, a bowl of water, and a little plate for mixing colors. They were urged to experiment with colors and brush strokes, using the bowls of water to moisten the colors and to clean their brushes.

But it didn't take more than one or two dips of the brush for the water in the bowls to turn a murky gray—what the teacher called a "shadow color." And once the water was dirty, it contaminated the brighter colors. The yellows were especially vulnerable; one touch of the dark water, and the sunny yellow water-color cake turned an ugly blackish-green.

What they needed, of course, was fresh water. So the teacher and the parent helpers began a process of moving around the room, systematically emptying the bowls and refilling the bowls with fresh water. It was a never-ending task, since the first bowls were dirty again long before the last bowls were refilled. And a few of the children didn't want their bowls refilled; they *liked* turning their paintings into muddy quag-mires of brown and black. But most of the children were thrilled with the clean water, and they painted with zest, producing colorful original creations.

I've learned that forgiveness works that way, too.

I hold up my cup to be filled with sparkling clean forgiveness. And almost immediately, the resentment is creeping in—shadowy grudges from past dark memories or anger at new slights. The process of emptying out the resentment and being filled with forgiveness is an ongoing one. It has to happen again and again—as Jesus told his disciples, "seventy times seven."

Sometimes I don't want to let go of my resentment; I grow fond of my dark, murky attitudes. But when I allow an infilling of fresh "water," I am set free to live a full, creative life.

Interestingly enough, forgiveness works this way in our lives whether we're the forgivers or the "forgivees." Actually, the distinction is not all that clear, because every one of us has need to be both. Like the colors in a watercolor painting, forgiving and being forgiven run together, creating surprising and unforgettable patterns.

Every single one of us, because we are human and sinful and make mistakes and act out of motives that are less than pure, has a continual need to ask forgiveness of God and other humans.

Every single one of us, because the people around us are human and sinful and make mistakes and act out of motives that are less than pure, has constant need to forgive—or to ask God for the ability to forgive.

(We need to ask because all forgiveness—whether offered or received—is a gift of God. I can no more muster honest forgiveness on my own than my favorite teacup can fill itself with apple-cinnamon tea.)

Forgiveness, then, is an ongoing process of filling our leaky little cups. But that isn't the whole story. Forgiveness is ongoing, but it's not an endless, repetitive cycle. Instead, forgiveness has a forward motion. It's more like a couple gracefully waltzing across the room than a dog chasing its tail.

Things change as we practice the process of forgiveness. Over time, specific hurts lose their power to hurt us (and some hurts really are healed at the moment of forgiveness). More important, emptying out anger becomes a habit. We become less likely to let hurts fester, and we become more careful of the feelings of others. More and more we grow to understand what it's like to lead a clean life. Forgiving, and being forgiven, we waltz forward along in the paths of righteousness.

My friend who helped with the art class did not have to go around emptying water bowls forever. By the time she had made several rounds, the children were learning to wipe their brushes before dipping them in the water. Beautiful pictures were emerging on the papers—a purple whale swimming in a sunset sea, a fat orange pumpkin smiling on an emerald lawn, a swirling pattern of purple and blue designs. As more paintings neared completion, there were fewer bowls to be emptied. Some of the kids who were finished even started helping with the cleanup. The class was moving along.

We never, in this life, reach a point where we don't need to forgive.

We never reach a point where we don't need forgiveness.

But we do, if we are depending on God, move closer to completion, closer to that beautiful picture he wants to paint in the world through us. We move closer to him, and we learn to follow him better.

Forgiveness is a ongoing process, but it's not an endless cycle.

I need to remember that today, because I am struggling to forgive someone I love very much. She has done some things I don't approve of, and she has hurt others whom I also love. I know that I need to forgive her, and I also need forgiveness for ways I have acted toward her. And I know this forgiveness won't come in an easy, once-and-for-all act. The hurt is too deep, the pain too immediate.

But I know forgiveness can happen, and I know the pain can heal, and I know that I can move closer and closer to forgiveness.

I know, because of what happened with my attitude toward my dad.

You see, despite the dark cloud in my soul that darkened the breakfast sunshine that morning with Bob, I really was learning to fill my cup with forgiveness. And when I read that difficult question from the jar, I felt some pain, but I did have an answer.

What would I do if I could spend a day with my dad?

First of all, I would take his hand, and we would walk and talk. "Remember, daddy?" I would say, and we would reminisce about when I was a little girl. "Remember the times you would set me up on the counter next to you while you worked? Remember when you'd take me through those big doors into the kitchens full of those great, shining pots and pans?" I always felt so proud when my daddy would introduce me to the chefs as his little girl. I always felt so safe when he held my hand.

"And, oh, daddy, I'm so sorry!" I'd tell my dad if I could spend a day with him. "I'm sorry for all the terrible things that happened to you, all the things that hurt you and made you the way you were." And I'd say, "Daddy, I know why you drank. I know why you were full of fury. You had so much pain in your heart, in your cup—from being abandoned when your parents died and being raised in the kitchen in the palace of Vienna. And you have so much pain from being a Jew in Nazi-occupied Austria, and having to change your name to escape, and fighting in the war and being shot three times."

Daddy used to show us the scars from those gunshot wounds, but it was the deeper, hidden scars that caused him more pain. In so many ways his life was nothing but a battle. No wonder he tried to blot it out with alcohol.

If I could spend a day with my dad, I wouldn't want to deny the pain that he caused me. It was real, and I've learned that denying real pain hinders forgiveness instead of helping it. But I would also want to tell my dad that I love him. I would want to thank him for what he gave me—my creativity, my talent with food, the love he poured on me when he wasn't drinking.

And more than anything else, I would want to tell my dad that we have a heavenly Father who can cover the hurt and pain and take it from us. I would want him to know, more than anything else, my dearest friend, the Messiah, the Lord Jesus, the One who said, "Forgive, and you will be forgiven" (Luke 6:37).

I can't do that, of course. I can't spend another day with my dad, and that will always be a source of sadness for me. But I know I have finally come to a place in my life where memories of him are no longer a source of bitterness for me. Forgiveness has finally cleansed the area of my heart where those memories reside. And because that is true, I am more confident that other areas can be cleansed as well. Because I know forgiveness works, I am more ready to waltz another round.

Forgiveness works, even when you can't tell it's working. Even when you don't feel forgiven or don't feel forgiving. Even when you don't particularly want to forgive, when you find yourself grumping to God, "All right, I'll forgive since you say so, but . . ."

And forgiveness works no matter what the forgiveness issues are in your life.

Perhaps your spouse has been unfaithful or your son has adopted a lifestyle you cannot approve. Perhaps a friend has said something cruel behind your back or a colleague has attacked you publicly. Perhaps you are struggling with ongoing bitterness over something that happened years ago.

Or perhaps you need forgiveness for yourself. Perhaps you are overwhelmed with guilt or simply miserable because a relationship has been ruptured. Perhaps you are furious with yourself over a thoughtless remark, or you are beginning to be convicted of a hidden sin that is keeping you from fellowship with God.

Whatever in your life is causing you pain, you don't need to let resentment fill your cup. Above all, you don't need to hold on to the bitter brew.

Forgiveness works. You can take your cup to the Lord and ask him to empty it of resentment and guilt, to fill it with sparkling forgiveness. In Christ you can find the strength, if it's appropriate, to go to the other people involved and ask for forgiveness—and you can find the grace to accept forgiveness from God if the other person is not ready to grant it. Even if the other people involved are no longer in your life—or no longer living—you can write them a letter and pour out your heart. Do whatever it takes to remove the cloud and cleanse your soul and set you again on the paths of rightness.

Be prepared to do it again, if necessary—even seventy times seven times. But remember that if you've asked, God has answered. First John 1:9 assures us, "If we confess our sins, He is faithful and just to forgive us our sins and to cleanse us from all unrighteousness."

This is so vital to remember in those times when, for one reason or another, the forgiveness doesn't seem to be working.

I know of a woman who went through a bad time in her marriage and made a series of painful mistakes. She fell apart emotionally, the marriage split up, and her husband was granted custody of their two young children. Although she wrote them faithfully, they were very angry and wanted nothing to do with her.

Unfortunately, her ex-husband was very bitter and inflamed these feelings of anger. Eventually he moved them to a state so distant that she could barely afford to visit (although she tried).

During all this time, the woman worked very hard to rebuild her life. She relied on a competent counselor and support groups. She also returned to the faith she had left behind many years earlier. On her knees she expressed her repentance to God and begged forgiveness for her part in all that had happened. She also wrote her children and asked their forgiveness for anything she had done to hurt them.

After that, the problems continued. Her ex-husband was still hostile, and he even used her requests for forgiveness to try to deny her visitation. Her children were still distant. They were so far away that visits were a severe financial hardship. She struggled with guilt for what she had done and deep worry about her children's future.

So she went to her pastor with her pain.

"I've asked God to forgive me," she said. "And I really think he has. So why don't I feel forgiven? And why is everything still so hard?"

That wise pastor looked at her with great compassion. "If you've asked the Lord for forgiveness, he *has* forgiven you. So maybe what you need now is not forgiveness, but the grace to live with the consequences of your actions."

That has been a very helpful word for me during the times in my life when forgiveness just doesn't seem to work.

Forgiveness is not a superglue for broken relationships. It's not an eraser for hurtful remarks or painful memories. And forgiveness doesn't excuse us from having to cope with the consequences of sin in our lives and the lives of others.

Forgiveness works, but it works at the soul level, sometimes deeper than we can see. And that is why forgiveness doesn't seem to change anything—at least not right away.

True forgiveness—given or received—works because it changes me.

But that, of course, changes everything.

Savoring God's Word . . . A Taste of Forgiveness

The kingdom of heaven is like a certain king who wanted to settle accounts with his servants. And when he had begun to settle accounts, one was brought to him who owed him ten thousand talents. But as he was not able to pay, his master commanded that he be sold, with his wife and children and all that he had, and that payment be made. The servant therefore fell down before him, saying, "Master, have patience with me, and I will pay you all." Then the master of that servant was moved with compassion, released him, and forgave him the debt. But that servant went out and found one of his fellow servants who owed him a hundred denarii; and he laid hands on him . . . , saying, "Pay me what you owe!" So his fellow servant fell down at his feet and begged him, saying, "Have patience with me, and I will pay you all." And he would not, but went and threw him into prison till he should pay the debt. So when his fellow servants saw what had been done, they were very grieved, and came and told their master all that had been done. Then his master, after he had called him, said to him, "You wicked servant! I forgave you all that debt because you begged

me. Should you not also have had compassion on your
fellow servant, just as I had pity on you?"

Matthew 18:23–33

Have mercy upon me, O God,
According to Your lovingkindness;
According to the multitude of Your tender mercies,
Blot out my transgressions.
Wash me thoroughly from my iniquity,
And cleanse me from my sin. . . .
Behold, You desire truth in the inward parts,
And in the hidden part You will make me to know wisdom.
Purge me with hyssop, and I shall be clean;
Wash me, and I shall be whiter than snow. . . .
Hide Your face from my sins,
And blot out all my iniquities.
Create in me a clean heart, O God,
And renew a steadfast spirit within me.
Do not cast me away from Your presence,
And do not take Your Holy Spirit from me.
Restore to me the joy of Your salvation,
And uphold me with Your generous Spirit.
Then I will teach transgressors Your ways,
And sinners shall be converted to You.

Psalm 51: 1-13

Fill my cup, Lord . . .

I offer you my cup of fear

and worry and overcontrol

that you may fill it with trust.

4

A Cup of Trust

*Yea, though I walk through the valley
of the shadow of death,
I will fear no evil . . .
Psalm 23:3*

One day Bob and I were in our van, trying to cross a really busy highway. There was no traffic light at this particular intersection, and the cars were whizzing by right and left. Bob was craning his neck, trying to find an opening. I didn't want to add to his worries, so I just sat quietly.

We sat there for several minutes with Bob poised to make his move. Finally he saw his opening and zipped out across the road. We made it!

As we continued on our way, Bob looked over at me. "You know, Em, I noticed you weren't even looking at all those cars. Weren't you worried we wouldn't get across?"

"Oh," I said without thinking, "I trust you."

Bob's questioning expression turned into a beaming smile. "Thank you," he said.

I was a little surprised by his enthusiastic response. But when I thought about it a little more, I understood why he was so pleased.

You see, trust is a compliment. It's a gesture of respect, a gift of esteem. And it's a gift not lightly given, because trust is also a risk. Trusting someone means giving that person a little bit of control over our lives—which means that other person may let us down.

That's why the trust of a child is so poignant. When a little one reaches up and takes my hand, I feel a little tug at my heartstrings because I know she's giving me the gift of her trust. She's trusting that I will help her and not hurt her, that I will meet her needs. Then I feel a surge of responsibility, because I know just how vulnerable that little child is. And I also feel a little stab of pain because I know this world can be so untrustworthy.

"Hey, trust me." Can you even hear the words without feeling a tingle of distrust? These days it seems we're bombarded with all the bad things that can happen if we let down our guard and trust *anybody*. We can be bilked or conned. We can be cheated, mugged, even murdered.

And we don't even need to leave home to be let down. Anyone who has ever lived in a relationship knows that. A promise broken, a responsibility shirked, a word spoken or not spoken—friends and families can betray each other with devastating accuracy. We do it out of carelessness, out of cruelty, out of our own mistrust.

I can still taste the bitter cup of betrayal and disappointment and fear I drank as a young girl growing up with an alcoholic father. I knew that my daddy loved me, but I couldn't trust him to control himself, to be consistent with me. I couldn't even trust him to go on living. Daddy died when I was eleven—and to a child, the death of a parent feels like abandonment, the ultimate betrayal.

I also knew the agony of trust when one of my uncles violated my body. "Come sit with me," he would say, and when I obeyed he would begin fondling me. Eventually I would get up and leave the room. I don't know why I didn't kick or scream or tell my aunt—perhaps because I had been raised to obey all adults. But I still remember that deep sense of betrayal when someone I trusted hurt me.

But you don't need my stories to convince you it's an untrustworthy world. You have your own stories. You know what it is like to be betrayed by those to whom you gave the gift of your trust. And you know you have to "be careful out there."

And yet, not trusting is not an option—if we want to have any relationships at all. We can't be close to anyone without giving that person the gift of our trust. We have to take the risk, even when we know we could be hurt.

The crucial questions, of course, are who and how. Whom can I trust? And how can I manage to trust again when my trust has been betrayed?

When it comes to people, there aren't any guarantees. We can be wise when it comes to choosing the people we relate to, trusting in our own instincts and the counsel of others and the nudging of the Holy Spirit. We can follow some commonsense precautions—like letting relationships develop slowly and not giving credit card numbers to people who call—to keep from becoming involved with extremely untrustworthy people. But even those precautions can't keep us truly safe.

The trouble is that *everyone* is untrustworthy at one time or another. We *all* let each other down. So I think we need to look a little deeper when it comes to choosing whom and how we are going to trust.

When it comes to people, I think we need to look at character and intentions—and what we are trusting others to be and do.

You see, I do trust my husband, Bob. I trust him profoundly. And yet I don't trust him never to make a mistake. I don't trust him never to hurt my feelings or forget an appointment or utter an unkind word. I don't trust my Bob not to be human. If I did, I would be setting myself up for long-term disappointment and bitterness.

What I do trust is Bob's fundamental character. I trust him to be the kind and competent man I know him to be. I trust him to want to stay in relationship with me, to want the best for me. I trust him to learn from his mistakes and to continue to grow.

And how do I know what Bob's character is like and what his intentions are? He's shown me! Over and over again in our life together he has shown that he can be trusted. Even before I met him or knew him well, I knew him by reputation. Mutual friends assured me that he was "all right." I also believe the Holy Spirit was working in my heart, softening it and allowing me to trust in the man God had chosen for me.

All of this brings me to the issue of trusting God. And sometimes I think it's a lot harder for me to trust God than it is to trust an imperfect (but wonderful) human like Bob. After all, God is a spirit. I can't touch him or smell him or see him. Like most people, I have my moments when I doubt he even exists.

And yet I need to trust God if I am going to live in relationship with him. I need to trust God in order to trust anyone else—for how else can I have the security to give the gift of my trust to people I know might let me down?

So how can I trust God?

Basically, it works with God the way it works with Bob.

I trust God because of what he is like, because of what he has done. And I know these things both from my own experience and from what I have seen in the lives of others. I can trust God because he has shown me who he is and what his intentions are toward me and all his people. Over and over, by his Word and his actions, he has shown that he is a God who can be trusted.

The holy Scriptures give dramatic witness to God's trustworthiness. The psalmist and the prophets and the gospels say it in pictures. The Lord is my rock. He is my help and shield. He is my redeemer. He is the bread of life, the living water, the good shepherd, the way and the truth and the life.

The Scriptures say it in story, too. Once upon a time there was a God who created human beings and chose a specific group of people to belong to him and show him to the world. Over the centuries this God cared for his people and rescued them and disciplined them and persistently loved them even when they turned their backs on him. And then this God made the ultimate commitment, passed the ultimate test of character and intent. He sent his only son to die for those people—to show us just how deeply he can be trusted.

To me the most incredible part in this whole incredible scriptural story is that I'm part of it. I, too, am created and rescued and disciplined and loved and redeemed by God. I, too, have a part in God's story. And my part is, in essence, to trust him, to let him work in my life and change me and guide me.

This really is a God I can trust. He's shown me by what he has done in the lives of so many people I know. Again and again, in the face of pain and doubt and despair, my God has proved himself trustworthy—I've seen it happen.

I think of my friend Carol Thornburg, who lost her beloved husband five years ago. They were so close, and she was so dependent on him, and I wondered how she would ever learn to function alone. But what a privilege it has been to see the ways God has provided for my friend through the years. He has taken her step-by-step from selling a house to buying a house to selling a house to being financially comfortable enough to volunteer her time in Christian ministry. In the five years she has been on her own, so she has learned to trust the Lord for her needs. And she has figured it out so that she has just enough money to live on while she gives away her time in the Lord's work.

And I think of others as well. Marilyn Heavilyn, who lost three sons and almost lost a grandbaby yet has touched so many through her testimony to God's goodness. Or Joni Eareckson Tada, who became a quadriplegic as a teenager but who speaks and writes and draws and sings so eloquently about God's goodness. Or Janis Willis, whose six children were killed in a highway accident but who managed to say, "I realized I had been saying, 'no, no, no,' to God as my children were entering heaven's doors. I was saying 'no God' to the very thing I ultimately wanted most for our children—to be with God eternally. . . . We have thrown ourselves into God's grace."[1]

And of course my own experience reminds me again and again that God can be trusted. Again and again in my life he has given me exactly what I needed in order to grow and move toward him.

This is a God who took a little girl with good reason to distrust men and healed that distrust by giving her a husband who is strong and dependable and nurturing.

This is a God who took a willing but inexperienced young wife and put her in charge of a household of five small children—an effective crash course in home organization—then gave her the opportunity and the encouragement to teach others what she had learned.

This is a God who took a restless empty-nest mom and gave her a nationwide ministry of writing and speaking.

And this is a God who, again and again, has given me the gift of his presence when I gave him the gift of my trust. When I look back at the way my life has unfolded, I can only be astonished at the wisdom and creativity of my heavenly Father.

This really is a God I can trust. In my life he has shown me again and again that he is a rock and a help and a shield, the way and the truth and the life.

And that raises another question.

Why do I still have such a hard time trusting God?

Why do I keep falling back into paralyzing fears and agonizing worries—as if God can't take care of me? Why do I keep trying to control my circumstances and my loved ones—as if God can't take care of them as well as me? Why do I keep acting as if this great trustworthy God were not capable of running the universe?

This last kind of distrust has always been a trap for me. Maybe it comes from having so much responsibility in my young life or from learning to be distrustful. But I tend to want everything to be right and good and perfect, and if things aren't running the way I think they should I tend to move in and take over. Do I want to control other people's lives when they're not moving in the direction I think they should?

No, I don't think that consciously. I just act that way. I've done it again and again in my life—given God my trust and then taken it back and tried to run things myself.

But I am learning. I am moving forward in my ability to trust. And God is helping me do it.

You see, what I am learning is that although my trust is a gift I offer to God, I cannot offer it unless he gives it to me first. He is the source from whom all blessings flow; I cannot offer him anything he didn't originate. And yet my offering is very important.

It's like a small child buying a gift for her mother. Where does the money come from the first place? Even if she draws her mother a picture, the crayons and the paper and even the little girl's talent came from the mother. And yet the act of giving brings such joy to both mother and child—and the child is learning valuable lessons at the same time.

So I give what I can. I offer to this great, trust-worthy God my cup of fear and worry and overcontrol. As I hold it up to him, my cup is emptied and filled with trust and handed back to me—so I can offer it back to him. And then I must offer my cup of trust back to him.

But I don't want to get too caught up in pretty pictures here. How specifically do I hold up my cup to be filled with trust?

One way is through prayer. I need to be offering up my cup daily in the form of prayer for my family, for my church, for my children. I need to pray that they will fear the Lord and serve him. And then—this is the hardest part—I need to relinquish them, to give over those concerns to the Lord as a gesture of trust. I need to learn to pray, "God, I pray that you will do whatever it takes to transform our son or daughter or grandchild into a person who will serve you, know you, and love you with all his heart, mind, and soul. I don't know what we will have to experience before that happens. But that is my prayer."

So prayer is an offering of trust, a way to hold up my cup for filling with more trust. So is patience, being willing to wait, even when the urge to take over is strong.

I have always found it especially hard to trust God when I think something should be happening—and it isn't. Those times really tend to throw me. But I'm gradually learning to trust God even in those maddening waiting times. I've been able to look back and see that during some of those times when God didn't seem to be moving, I was moving in growth. Or I can see that if God had acted when I wanted him to, things would not have turned out so well; God's timing was far better than mine.

This brings me back again to trusting that God knows best, that he is capable of running the universe. When I wait patiently for the Lord to act in his own time, I am giving him the gift of my trust—and growing in my ability to trust.

Most of the time, though, it's not just a matter of waiting. Obedience—the willingness to follow God's nudges even when we don't completely understand why—is crucial. It's no accident that the old hymn was titled "Trust and Obey." They go together. And they're both hard. In fact, without God, they're impossible. Our cups are empty of all good things unless God is filling them.

But God does fill our cups when we hold them up. I'm learning that more and more these days. The recent unhappiness in my family has made me realize how weak my trust can be and how desperately I want to trust God. I am really seeking to trust him in every area of my life, from what happens in the next five minutes to what happens in the next five years.

And you know, the more I trust him, the more I'm learning to trust. The more I'm coming to know his character, to stare in amazement at what he's done in my life and wait in anticipation for what he's going to do next. I'm learning the truth that C. W. Christian expressed so eloquently:

My faith is small.
I measure it in dust
And test its weight with straw
And wonder that he pays me heed at all.
How well I must
In my self-serving supplication gall
His patience with my feeble trust.
Yet I in all fair expectation wait.
My faith is small;
My God is great.[2]

So I am learning a lot more about trust these days, and as a result, my life is much more peaceful. I also find that my perspective has sharpened; I have a clearer sense of the basic realities. I know who I can trust—and how.

I can trust God to care for me and help me grow. I can trust God to give me his presence in this life and then, when my life is over, to take me home to glory.

Most important, I can trust God to run the universe. (I don't have to.) That trust enables me to take a more lighthearted attitude toward all that concerns me.

Take my teacups, for instance.

The collection of teacups in my armoire and all around the house is one of my signatures—one of the things I'm known for. I've spoken about my teacups, and written about them. They are full of memories and very precious to me, and I've always been very protective of them. But a few years ago I realized that my time was more valuable. To write or speak or minister, I needed to relinquish my house to someone who could clean for me. Relinquishing the task of cleaning the armoire with the teacups was the hardest. How could I trust anyone else with my precious collection?

Well, not long after I gave up the task, my fears were realized. The housekeeper put the shelf back in wrong; it slipped and broke some of the teacups. That was a traumatic day. But when I took my pain to God, trusting him with it, he gently and gradually changed my attitude.

I still love my teacups, but I'm not nearly as vigilant about them anymore. Now I reassure my housekeeper, "Don't be afraid of the teacups." (And I know she is more careful with them than I am.) Now I'm more likely to let little children drink tea out of my cups, to give them the gift of my trust along with the assurance that an accident won't cause me to love them any less.

For many years I have had tea parties with my granddaughter, Christine. Her brothers Chad and Bevan have enjoyed their tea parties, too. And recently when our little two-and-a-half-year-old Bradley Joe was over at the house I had a tea party with him, trusting him to drink very carefully out of one of my china teacups. I knew he could easily break that delicate cup. But I wanted to take that risk to show him how special he was to me. And he got the message. He went home and told his mother excitedly about his grownup tea party with Grammy. Even in his baby mind, he sensed he was being trusted and he tried his best to live up to it.

And that gives me a little insight, too, into how my relationship with God works—how he fills my cup with trust.

This most trustworthy God teaches me to trust—by trusting me!

Remember, real trust is a gift you give to someone you love. It's a compliment, a gesture of respect. And it's also a way of helping them grow, to become more trustworthy.

Or put another way, when I choose to live in relationship with someone, I have to give the gift of my trust—or it's not really a relationship, just a contract.

If an employee embezzles or doesn't show up for work, it hurts the employer in the pocketbook. If that employee is also a friend, if you have a relationship, the embezzlement or absence is a betrayal of trust.

You don't have trust unless you have a relationship.

And because he wants a relationship with me, the trustworthy God who created the universe has trusted me to do his work in the world!

He has entrusted me with a family and friends and charged me with living in a way that helps them draw close to them. He has entrusted me with the job of ministry—with the women I speak to and the people who read my books and also the people I meet in the course of my everyday life. He has entrusted me with his love so that I can have a relationship with him and with others.

Do I abuse that trust?

Of course. I do it every day.

I abuse God's trust whenever I ignore one of those little nudgings of the Holy Spirit to go see someone or help someone. I abuse his trust when I snap at Bob or criticize one of my children. I abuse his trust when I fail to trust him.

But that's sort of beside the point because, in this world, if trust depended on trust never being betrayed—we'd never trust anybody. If I waited until I was sure the grandchildren would never break a teacup, I would never have a tea party with them.

Trusting is a risk you take in the interest of love. It's a calculated gamble, risking betrayal in the interest of the other person's growth. You don't necessarily trust that the other person won't do wrong, but you do trust that the person will stay in relationship with you and grow. You trust that person's basic character and potential. You trust who the person is, and who the person can be.

And that's what God does with us. The very fact that we have a life is an astounding vote of confidence on God's part. The fact that we have free will is an amazing act of trust. He's trusting that we will come to him! He's giving us room to grow.

When I was a little girl, I would sometimes wake up in the middle of the night and need to go to the bathroom. It was dark. We didn't have a night-light. So I would call out in the darkness.

"Mama, I need to go."

"Well, then, go," she would answer, her voice close and warm.

"But it's dark. I'm afraid."

Her reply came gently, assuring me of her presence, trusting me to grow.

"Be afraid," she would say, "but go."

More and more, as I grow older, I've become aware of God's love and trust working like that in my life. He allows the pain and the fear and the struggle because he trusts me to grow through them. But he's always present, a comforting, trustworthy voice in the darkness, telling me:

"Be afraid, but go. There is no place you can go that I won't be.

"Go ahead," he says. "You can trust me."

And I can.

Savoring God's Word . . .
A Taste of Trust

You will keep him in perfect peace, whose mind is stayed on You, because he trusts in You.

Isaiah 26:3

I will both lie down in peace, and sleep; for You alone,
O Lord, make me dwell in safety.

Psalm 4:8

The Lord is my strength and my shield;
My heart trusted in Him, and I am helped;
Therefore my heart greatly rejoices,
And with my song I will praise Him.

Psalm 28:7

Not that we are sufficient of ourselves to think of anything as being from ourselves, but our sufficiency is from God.

2 Corinthians 3:5

"Ah, Lord God! Behold, You have made the heavens and the earth by Your great power and outstretched arm. There is nothing too hard for You.

Jeremiah 32:17

Consider the lilies of the field, how they grow; they neither toil nor spin; and yet I say to you that even Solomon in all his glory was not arrayed like one of these. Now if God so clothes the grass of the field, which today is, and tomorrow is thrown into the oven, will He not much more clothe you, O you of little faith? Therefore do not worry, saying, 'What shall we eat?' or 'What shall we drink?' or 'What shall we wear?' For after all these things the Gentiles seek. For your heavenly Father knows that you need all these things. But seek first the kingdom of God and His righteousness, and all these things shall be added to you."

Matthew 6:28-33

Do not fret because of evildoers,
Nor be envious of the workers of iniquity....
Trust in the Lord, and do good;
Dwell in the land, and feed on His faithfulness.
Delight yourself also in the Lord,
And He shall give you the desires of your heart.
Commit your way to the Lord,
Trust also in Him,
And He shall bring it to pass.
He shall bring forth your righteousness as the light,
And your justice as the noonday.
Rest in the Lord, and wait patiently for Him....
For evildoers shall be cut off;
But those who wait on the Lord,
They shall inherit the earth.

Psalm 37

Fill my cup, Lord . . .

I offer you my cup of loneliness and

selfishness, that you may

give me your cup of communion.

5

A Cup of Communion

You are with me.

Psalm 23:4

$\mathcal{I}$t's one of my favorite times of day.

The sun has set. The phone has stopped ringing.
(I hope!) The conference schedules are filed away, and
the dishwasher is finishing up the last of the mealtime
chores. A little fire in the fireplace chases away the
chill, while a string quartet plays merrily on the CD.

Bob is comfortable in his big green leather easy
chair, an afghan on his lap and a book in his hand.
Every few minutes he stops to read me a passage
while I putter in the kitchen, preparing our evening
cup of tea.

I don't hurry as I pour the boiling water into the
teapot. The delightful scent of cinnamon starts to waft

around the kitchen as I gather together lace napkins, china cups, sugar, and cream. A candle in a crystal holder casts a golden glow, a single daisy plucked from an arrangement in the hall smiles from a miniature vase. I rummage quietly in the pantry to find a few cookies, and I know there's a bunch of grapes in the refrigerator.

The tea is steeped. I carry the tray into our peaceful living room.

Bob moves his feet from the hassock to make room for the tray. I curl up on the carpet beside him and pour. And then while the fire crackles and the music dances, we talk quietly or we pray or we just sit and share our cup of cinnamon and sharing—our delicious cup of communion.

Communion, you see, is not just another name for the Lord's Supper—although the ritual of bread and wine embodies that reality on the most profound level.

Communion is also the appropriate word for what happens whenever spirits are shared and cups are filled with love and mutual participation. It's what happens whenever human beings draw near to each other and to God, managing somehow to emerge from their separateness and partake of the shared life God intended.

You see, God never intended for us to be alone. He said that from the beginning. He made us for each other and for fellowship with him.

Our separateness, our deep-seated loneliness, that familiar sense of being all alone in a body with "me, me, me"—that's our own doing. It's the long-term result of that long-ago choice to listen to a serpent, eat an apple, take charge of our own destiny. Because we are sinful, there's a part of us that always wants to hide from God and each other.

And then we feel so alone, even in the midst of a crowd. Even in the bustle of our work, the warmth of our families. By ourselves we are just ourselves, and our cups are full of ourselves only.

That's why those moments of true communion are so delicious. They are a pure gift, a generous outpouring from the God whose very nature is relationship. (For what is the holy Trinity but an intertwined relationship of three identities—Father, Son, and Holy Spirit?) It is my loving Lord who empties my cup of loneliness and selfishness and pours for me my cup of communion.

That doesn't mean that people who don't know God cannot enjoy moments of special sharing or even deep connection. It doesn't mean you have be a Christian in order to enjoy closeness and friendship. In a sense, the cup of communion is a gift from creation, part of how we are made. God created us to connect to each other, and even our sinful separation has not negated that built-in capacity. God made us with the need for other people and the desire to live in harmony instead of discord, sharing instead of separation, fulfillment instead of loneliness. He created us with the physical and emotional tools we need to connect with each other—eyes, hands, voices, sympathy, loyalty, understanding. Human beings do manage to make some connections with each other while living apart from God.

And yet there is something so different, something so special about the cup of communion that is poured for me when I bring my cup of loneliness to the throne of God and hold it up to be washed and refilled with sharing and closeness and love. It's like the difference between muddy pond water and water from a flowing spring. It sparkles.

That's why, although I may have good and even loving relationships with men and women who don't know Christ—and there are many in my family—the relationships I share with my Christian brothers and sisters are different. It's more than just having a belief or a cause in common. It's having a *life* in common. When even two or three of us are gathered in the Lord's name, the presence of the Holy Spirit adds a sparkling eternal dimension to our human communion.

I cannot even begin to imagine what our marriage would be like without that eternal dimension. My Bob, who is very wise, knew from the beginning that we would have little chance of going the distance without having a closeness in that area. Even though he was attracted to me and respected my Jewish heritage, he held back. Instead of courting me, he shared his faith with me. And only when we had come to share a commitment to Jesus Christ as the Messiah did he propose marriage.

Over and over in my life I have thanked the Lord for Bob's strength and wisdom, for we have needed the spiritual communion of our shared faith to get through the tough times in our life together. My husband has always been my best friend, and being able to pray together and read Scripture together and talk together about the Lord and work together in ministry has been a privilege and a joy. In my marriage, God has poured out his cup of communion with overflowing generosity.

And there are other ways God fills my cup with communion. I have always loved sharing my faith with our children and especially with the grandchildren. I love to see them growing in the Lord, even through their painful experiences. In many ways they minister to me, and I rejoice to see that they have a spiritual foundation I never had at their age.

My church family, too, offers me so many opportunities to come out of my loneliness and share a cup of communion. Bob and I have developed deep and meaningful friendships in this body. I love the sense of spiritual sharing I feel when we sing and study and serve together, and especially when we gather together at the Lord's table to remember his ultimate act of sharing.

Even closer to my heart than my church family is my special adopted family of prayer partners. These are my close-to-the-heart friends whose love has stood the test of time. These are the people I call when my heart is aching, the ones I trust above all others to pray with me. They are all so different—Yoli and Barbara and Donna. But they are truly the sisters of my heart. They are the ones I trust not only with my tears, but with my puffy red eyes and unsightly runny nose and scrunched-up crying face. They have truly been God's gift of communion to me.

But my cup of communion is not just filled among the people I know. My kinship with other brothers and sisters in Christ has brought Bob and me into "family reunions" across the nation. This is one of the most amazing surprises God has given me over my lifetime (and there have been so many surprises!). He has used our ministry of teaching and writing not only to do his work of touching lives and reclaiming spirits, but also to fill our cups with sparkling Christian communion.

We are on the road nearly every week, traveling to lead seminars in towns we've never visited before. We've reached the point where we can almost predict what will happen. Someone we have never seen will meet us at the airport. For three or four days we will pray together and eat together and work together and perhaps live together with people with whom we may have little in common but a shared desire to serve the Lord. And then, by the time the weekend is over, our cup of communion will be filled. We are all fast friends. Sometimes we will end up being in touch for years.

It doesn't just happen with seminars, either. By God's grace, I have been able to share deeply with people I will never meet, women I encounter only as a voice on the phone or a face at a conference or a folded-up sheet of notepaper in an envelope. Somehow God uses what I say or do to touch these women. Somehow they find the courage to come to me with their pain. And somehow, as we talk together or pray together, he fills both our cups with a special kind of communion.

But perhaps you are a bit fed up by now with my litany of communion. Perhaps you are going through a lonely time. Perhaps you are grieving the loss of someone you loved or having difficulty making friends.

Perhaps you feel isolated and alone in the midst of your family or your church, and my stories about a close marriage or a loving church family or sympathetic friends just leave you feeling hollow.

I understand if you feel that way.

You see, the very reason my cups of communion seem so amazing is that my cup was very full of loneliness for most of my life. I am an introverted person by nature, and the pain of living in an alcoholic home wrapped me further in a shell of separateness. I grew up feeling different and alone, and I would never have considered bringing other children home to my disordered household. Then, after my father died, I was too busy trying to keep house for my mother and manage my schoolwork to have time for friends—even if I could come out of myself enough to make one.

And even though God in his amazing mercy has granted me the gift of a good marriage and good friendships, I don't always feel like my cup of communion is filled. There are many times when I struggle with a private grief in the midst of a public crowd. Sometimes I can be in church or with Bob and feel like I'm a million miles away. And I still find that my best friends are those who reach out to me first, those who don't wait for me to reach out to them.

My cup of communion—like so many of my "earthen vessel" cups—is a leaky one, and when the sharing drains away I often find I'm the same shy little girl who hid behind her mother's skirts.

I know I'm not the only one who feels this way. All of our cups are leaky when it comes to communion. Even though we were created for sharing, we are also flawed by the sin, and sin is separation—from God and from other human beings. We are made for relationships, but we are also selfish, and we suffer from the selfishness of others. We yearn to be close to others, but we are also lonely to the core, still locked inside our own skulls, unable on our own to truly understand or reach out.

So even though we were created for communion, communion is still a miracle.

Without the miracle of communion, friendships go flat, church friends betray each other, marriages dissolve into separateness or fall apart altogether. Without the miracle of communion I am left with only me. But with the miracle of communion I am filled.

And here's the biggest miracle of all. I don't have to make friends or influence people in order to have my cup filled with communion. I don't even need to be with other people.

Sometimes my heavenly Father does fill my cup of communion through my relationships with Bob or my children or my church or my prayer partners or the people who come to my seminars.

But always—with or without other people—he fills my cup of communion with himself. My most satisfying cup of sharing comes in my relationship with him.

I love the way Tracey St. John put it in her letter to a national columnist. Lynn Minton, in her column on youth in *Parade* magazine, had asked readers, "Do you believe in God?" This is what Tracey wrote:

I was 17 when I left high school, depressed and without direction. I found myself pregnant and married a man who essentially reaffirmed that I was not going to amount to much. I later divorced him and continued making monumentally lousy decisions.

Then I met someone, now my best friend. He too is a parent. He began to tell me that I was worth something. He listened as I expressed my disgust with what I had done with my life. At times, I even personally attacked him. But his patience was unbelievable. Today, I am a student in a very competitive medical program and a much better parent. I owe all my success to my best friend, who has been there every step of the way.

So what does this have to do with whether I believe in God? Who do you think my best friend is? *

My life has been different from Tracey's, but her experience with God has been my experience, too.

---

* Quoted in "Lynn Minton Reports: Fresh Voices," *Parade* (15 October 1995): 23.

Over the years, I have learned that Jesus is the One I can always trust, the One I can always talk to, the One whose love truly changes my life.

I know that I can talk to the Lord and say, "Today I'm not feeling that I can trust. Today I'm not sure that I like my Bob too much. Today I'm really upset with the children." The one thing I really have experienced with the Lord is that I can tell him anything, that he's not going to tell anybody else, and that he's going to comfort me and forgive and love me.

That's what a real friend is, isn't it?

A friend can love you in spite of who you are.

A friend can comfort you wherever you are.

A friend can speak to you in honesty but then encourage you to move on to the next step.

A friend can fill your cup with sharing and closeness and love—with communion.

The old hymn really had it right: "What a Friend We Have in Jesus."

The older I get, the more I long for that friendship with my Lord to grow. I realize there isn't any thing else on this earth that can give me more joy or fulfillment or strength. I want to talk with him, to share my life with him, to hold my cup of communion up to be filled with him. I want my Lord to use me, to live in me, to fill others' cups through me.

No, I don't always get it right. I don't always feel close to Jesus—anymore than I always feel close to Bob or our children or our fellow creatures. As long as I live in this sin-touched body and in this sin-touched world, my cup will leak.

That is why I must constantly pray—

Lord, I'm lonely. Fill my cup.

Lord, I've been so caught up in myself I can't even think about Bob or Jenny or Yoli or anybody else. Fill my cup.

Lord, I've been trying to do it all by myself again. I've been trying to go it on my own. And I don't want to do it anymore.

Fill my cup, Lord, with communion.

Fill my cup, Lord, with you.

Savoring God's Word . . .
A Taste of Communion

And the Lord God said, "It is not good that man should be alone."

Genesis 2:18

God sets the solitary in families;
He brings out those who are bound into prosperity;
But the rebellious dwell in a dry land.

Psalm 68:6

I say to you that if two of you agree on earth concerning anything that they ask, it will be done for them by My Father in heaven. For where two or three are gathered together in My name, I am there in the midst of them.

Matthew 18:19,20

The cup of blessing which we bless, is it not the communion of the blood of Christ? The bread which we break, is it not the communion of the body of Christ? For we, being many, are one bread and one body; for we all partake of that one bread.

I Corinthians 10:16,17

Jesus spoke these words, lifted up His eyes to heaven, and said, ". . . Holy Father, keep through Your name those whom You have given Me, that they may be one as We are. . . . I do not pray for these alone, but also for those who will believe in Me through their word; that they all may be one, as You, Father, are in Me, and I in You; that they also may be one in Us, that the world may believe that You sent Me."

John 17:1,11,20-22

No longer do I call you servants, for a servant does not know what his master is doing; but I have called you friends, for all things that I heard from My Father I have made known to you.

John 15:15

If we walk in the light as He is in the light, we have fellowship with one another, and the blood of Jesus Christ His Son cleanses us from all sin.

1 John 1:7

I thank my God upon every remembrance of you.

Philippians 1:3

Fill my cup, Lord . . .

I offer you my cracked and

crumbling cup

that you may remold me

and make me strong.

6

A Cup of Strength

Your rod and Your staff,
they comfort me.
Psalm 23:4

It was three o'clock in the afternoon on a day in early December. The chairs for our holiday seminar were being set up in the assembly hall. Our boxes and baskets of prayer planners and feather dusters and rubber "spootulas" were stacked behind the long tables, ready to be displayed and sold. Someone was on the stage, fiddling with the sound system. Someone else was putting up signs.

And me? I was in the process of coming unglued. Dissolving into tears. Totally losing it.

Now, hysterics are not normal for me, especially not right before a seminar. But I was drained from weeks of traveling, doing workshop after workshop in a series of different cities and churches. I was run-down from meeting people, giving to people, hauling books, and making bookings, and I was fighting a low-grade sinus infection that refused to go away. But I had really been looking forward to this seminar because it was here in our very own town, in our very own church, arranged for by people I knew and loved. This one was going to be easy and fun.

Then the woman in charge of the registration process called with a problem. Apparently we had overbooked the hall. Twelve hundred women had sent in their registration forms, and we had seats for only a thousand. The fire marshal had said no to putting in more chairs, so we would have to turn two hundred women away.

That little piece of bad news did it. My composure collapsed like a blob of warm jelly. All I could think of was those two hundred women.

"We can't turn them away," I sobbed. "God moved their hearts to want to come here; he must have a blessing for them. We can't turn them away from getting a blessing. Maybe there's somebody who really needs to be here tonight. We can't turn anybody away. We just can't . . ."

Without a word our friend Ellen, who helps us in our office and at our seminars, stepped close and took me in her arms. She pressed my head against her shoulder and murmured the way you do to a baby who is out of control.

"There, there, it's going to be all right."

And you know what? It was all right.

Ellen was God's strength to me at that moment. I leaned on her until I calmed down and regained control. Meanwhile, someone stepped in and began making plans for handling the overflow. Seats were found for the extra two hundred people. We even were able to accommodate two women from Oregon who just happened to walk in—although they literally had to sit in the bathroom and watch the seminar on closed-circuit TV.

I completed that weekend with an unusual sense of fulfillment and blessing. Not only did I sense God's presence in a special way during the sessions, but I was also profoundly grateful to Ellen and the others for ministering to me in a moment when life was just too much. And I was reminded in a vivid way of a truth I often want to ignore:

I don't have to be strong all the time.

In fact, God doesn't *want* me to be strong—at least not the way the world usually defines it.

God wants me to learn to lean on him the way I leaned on Ellen, the way a weary shepherd leans on his staff. He wants me to be comforted by his mighty power and to depend on him, not my jerky little efforts, to get through my life. He wants to fill my cup with the strong brew of his magnificent presence.

This is not a new insight. You've probably heard it before. You've heard that the Lord's strength is made perfect in weakness. It is. But what does that mean in terms of how we act and speak in our everyday lives?

Does God want us to *try* to be weak just so he can be strong?

No, that's not it at all. The point is not trying to be weak. The point is that we *are* weak.

We are cracked teacups, crumbling little earthenware creations, made in the divine image and gifted by God, but still weak, subject to breakage. We live in bodies that can break down. We are lazy, inconstant, stained with sin and selfishness, vulnerable to hate and pride and jealousy.

And God?

He is God! He is the creator of the universe, the One who keeps the galaxies whirling. He is the One who dreamed up blue whales and plankton, quantum physics and nuclear energy—and us. He was the One who opened the sea and raised Lazarus from the dead and then conquered death once and for all.

The simple little children's song sums it up succinctly:

> Little ones to him belong,
> They are weak but he is strong.

So the real issue here is not trying to be weak or strong, but getting a clear view of who we are and who God is.

The Bible doesn't tell us, "Be strong." And it doesn't tell us, "Be weak."

It tells us, "Look at who you are, and look at who God is." And then do the logical thing—which is to lean on him, to depend on his strength.

But it's not always easy to do. We are too brainwashed by the messages of the world: Be tough, get physical, command respect, don't let anyone walk all over you.

We're driven by fear, too. If we're not strong, we think, others will walk all over us. If we're not tough, we won't survive. We need our shell. We need our cocky confidence.

But here's another amazing paradox.

When we try to be strong on our own, we only end up showing how weak we really are. We become stiff and brittle or out of control. Even if we end up on top, we will eventually be toppled.

But when we take an alternate path, God's path, and let him be the strong one, an amazing thing happens. We admit our weakness and lean on him. And then . . . we become stronger.

I become a strong woman of God when I offer him my cup of weakness and ask him in all humility to fill it with his strength. What an incredible thought: The power that runs the universe is available to me if I am humble enough to accept it.

How do I experience that power? It depends on the situation.

First, God gives me strength to keep going during those times—like that memorable holiday seminar—when my strength gives out. This is almost like spiritual first aid. God may have a lesson for me to learn in the incident, or he may be telling me I need to slow down or make a change. But in the meantime, he often lends me an infusion of strength to carry me through.

Often the strength comes through other people. Ellen was God's strength to me in these awful moments before the holiday seminar. And my Bob has consistently been a source of strength to me in the course of our life together. I especially appreciate his strength and support after I've been on the platform all day and given out everything I know to give. When I feel that all my energy has been drained from my cup, that my strength is totally depleted, Bob will step in to pack up the materials and load the van and take me to dinner. Often he'll carry the conversation or just sit in silence because he understands that I'm all "talked out."

Bob does so much for me that I've always thought of him as "the strong one." But I've begun to realize that Bob and I take turns being strong for each other.

I've seen this with special clarity in the past few years, as we have struggled to cope with painful events in our family. We have rarely been weak at the same time. When Bob is really upset and doesn't feel he can tolerate what's going on, I seem to be handling the situation better or praying more consistently or keeping on a more even keel. Then, when I've had all I can take, Bob will be holding steady.

This is a natural rhythm. I've seen it work with employees in a business and with children in a family. And it works with non-Christians as well as Christians. But I think it is a rhythm God uses to help us. We take turns being God's strength to one another as we care for the people we love.

But God doesn't just work through loved ones in providing the infusions of strength I need to move forward. I've found he can be amazingly creative in supplying me with strength I need. I've had acquaintances or even strangers call me and say, "I'm not sure why I'm calling you, but I want you to know I'm praying for you." Sometimes when that has happened I hadn't even realized I had a need! But other times I knew exactly what the problem was. What a blessing to hear over the phone, "I don't need to know what you're going through; I just really feel that you need some strength from me."

But God's strength is not available just for crisis times. It is also available for my everyday life, for those ordinary days and weeks when nothing much seems to be happening. In those times I need strength to honor my commitments, to do what I ought to do, to keep from being worn down in the daily grind.

This kind of strength comes to me most dependably in my daily communion with God. When I am spending time in the Word and leaning on him in daily prayer, I am also growing stronger. Not only am I better able to handle my ordinary life today, I am also better equipped for tomorrow's crisis.

I find it works a little like that wonderful fabric stiffener you can buy in craft stores. The stiffener is used for making fabric bows that hold their shape without wilting—wonderful for decorating baskets and floral arrangements. To make a bow, you take a strip of fabric and soak it in the thick liquid until all the fibers have been permeated. Then you shape the bow and allow it to dry. The finished product is sturdy and flexible; bows made through this process are beautiful and shapely, and they don't sag or fray.

My times of communion with God work like that stiffener in my life. They soak the fibers of my being in the Lord's strength. When I spend time in prayer and meditation, when I read his Word or read what others have written about him, when I sing or praise or just try to spend time in his presence, I am soaking him up. In myself, I'm still that limp old cotton fabric. But when I have been permeated by him I have the capacity to be strong and resilient and beautiful.

But there's more to living in the Lord's strength than just "soaking" in Scripture and prayer. The actual process of becoming strong and beautiful takes a bit more energy. Growing strong in the Lord is not usually just a matter of sitting around and waiting until I'm strong so that *then* I can do what he wants me to do. More often, it's a matter of doing what I think God wants me to do, trusting that I will be given the strength I need when I need it.

In other words, God doesn't expect me to be strong. But he does expect me to be obedient.

And I have to say yes to his leading if I want to be a strong woman of God.

I have to follow up on the little nudges and the big messages he has sent me in my prayer times and during the day. I have to step forward, trusting that the

Lord who gave the orders will also provide the strength to carry them out.

And that, in turn, takes courage.

It takes courage to say yes to being weak, courage to say yes to the Lord's leading instead of depending on your own strength, courage to say, "I can't do it, Lord. But I'll still try if you go with me."

I have learned that the most amazing infusions of God's strength happen like that, when I am taking the risk of obeying God. So often in my life I have been astonished at how my Lord can take a tiny faith step and turn it into a strong leap for his kingdom.

It's a little like those moving sidewalks in a big airport.

These days, it seems that Bob and I spend half our lives in airports, so we loved this image, which came from my friend Anne's prayer group. (One of the group members even wrote a country-western song about it!)

Picture yourself walking down the concourse, lugging your shoulder bags and dragging your rolling cart behind you. Your boss has sent you on a special assignment, and your gate is at the very end of an impossibly long corridor. But just up ahead you spot the long black walkway with the handrails. It's the moving sidewalk.

A woman just a few paces ahead of you steps on. She's obviously very weak and weary, so she just grabs onto the handrail and lets the walkway carry her along.

Right after her is a businessman with no luggage but a briefcase. He's obviously not in a hurry. So he just steps onto the sidewalk and moves along at a regular pace. But the momentum of the moving panel does add an extra bounce to his step. You can tell because he's passing the people who decided not to take the walkway.

You don't have the leisure of a stroll down the concourse. You have a mission to accomplish, and you're already walking as fast as you can. Without slowing your pace, you take a big step onto the walkway. And whoosh! you feel the power. Now every step feels like a giant step, taken with less effort. You feel like you're in an old-fashioned sneaker commercial, running faster and jumping higher. The steps are yours, but the walkway is carrying you, too.

I often have that "whoosh" feeling when I step on a platform to speak. I am always in awe of the responsibility I have to the women in my audiences. And there are times when I am so weak, when I feel I don't have the energy to connect even with God. But I am convinced that this is where God wants me, so I go ahead and step on the platform. And in a matter of moments the Spirit of God will take over and strengthen me and give me the power I need to share myself and my Lord.

It doesn't always happen that way. Sometimes I feel pretty energetic and strong, and I may decide to go it on my own. I may decide to skip the moving sidewalk and just walk down the concourse myself. And sometimes I guess I do a pretty good job that way. But it's completely different when I'm relying on the Lord's strength, depending on him to do what needs to be done. I can almost feel the moment when I lean on the Lord and let his strength take over. Whoosh!

And although I've seen it again and again, I'm always amazed at what happens next. I will look out and see every eye glued on me, every ear tuned to the words coming out of my mouth. Sometimes I'll see tears running down cheeks. And then I'll think, "But this is just me—an ordinary housewife and mother with a high school education and a dysfunctional background and no training in speaking or writing. What am I doing here that would be so meaningful to them?"

I really am not trying to put myself down here. I know that God has made me special. But I also know that what happens in those seminars is so far beyond what I am capable of on my own that I can't take any of the credit. It's God's strength and the power of his Word coming through.

And that power and strength is available to you, no matter what your life is like, whether you're at the end of your rope or just moving along in an ordinary life or ready to take a big, risky step into ministry of some kind. The promise of God's strength doesn't apply just to speakers or writers or ministers. I have seen him at work in so many different lives, seen the amazing things that result when men and women give him their weakness and rely on his strength.

I think of a woman I know who has suffered emotional problems to the point of being in and out of mental hospitals. I can't imagine coping with the kind of pain she has endured. And yet she keeps moving forward, keeps holding out her cup to receive the Lord's strength. She uplifts me.

Or I think of friend whose only daughter has struggled with dyslexia, has had an abortion, has attempted suicide. My friend has agonized, worried, intervened. She has also had to cope with losing a house and with ongoing financial instability. Yet this is the friend who has taught me how to crawl up into the lap of my heavenly Father and find strength in his arms. She teaches me how to find strength in weakness.

I think of my strong Bob, who touches the lives of so many women in our seminars because he is willing to be open and vulnerable to them, to be honest about his feelings and weaknesses. He even lets me talk about him in my seminars—a position of weakness that requires enormous strength and courage. I have always loved and respected my Bob, but my respect has grown as I have observed his willingness to be weak in the Lord's service and have watched him grow stronger in the Lord's love.

I think of so many other people—young moms with children at home, dads whose teenagers are in trouble, people struggling with illness or working at jobs that sap their spirits. And these men and women are an example to me because I see them turning to the Lord in their pain and weakness. Turning to him when life seems too much or just too daily, or when the challenge is beyond them.

The simple child's song really is true.

We *are* weak.

But he *is* strong.

And his mighty arms are outstretched to us, ready to pour out his strength into our weak and fragile little cups.

And all we have to do is hold them up to him.

Savoring God's Word . . .
A Taste of Strength

The Lord is my light and my salvation;
Whom shall I fear?
The Lord is the strength of my life;
Of whom shall I be afraid? . . .
Wait on the Lord;
Be of good courage,
And He shall strengthen your heart;
Wait, I say, on the Lord!

Psalm 27:1, 14

Blessed is the man whose strength is in You, whose heart
is set on pilgrimage.

Psalm 84:5

He gives power to the weak, and to those who have no
might He increases strength. . . . But those who wait on
the Lord shall renew their strength; they shall mount up
with wings like eagles, they shall run and not be weary,
they shall walk and not faint.

Isaiah 40:29, 31

I have prayed for you, that your faith should not fail; and when you have returned to Me, strengthen your brethren.

Luke 22:32

The foolishness of God is wiser than men, and the weakness of God is stronger than men. For you see your calling, brethren, that not many wise according to the flesh, not many mighty, not many noble, are called. But God has chosen the foolish things of the world to put to shame the wise, and God has chosen the weak things of the world to put to shame the things which are mighty; and the base things of the world and the things which are despised God has chosen, and the things which are not, to bring to nothing the things that are, that no flesh should glory in his presence.

1 Corinthians 1:25-29

And He said to me, "My grace is sufficient for you, for My strength is made perfect in weakness." Therefore most gladly I will rather boast in my infirmities, that the power of Christ may rest upon me.

2 Corinthians 12:9

May the God of all grace, who called us to His eternal glory by Christ Jesus, after you have suffered a while, perfect, establish, strengthen, and settle you.

1 Peter 5:10

Fill my cup, Lord . . .

I offer my cup of pain—

the cup you know too well.

Fill my cup with thanksgiving and hope

that someday my cup of tears

will be filled with joy.

7

A Cup of Thanksgiving

You prepare a table before me
in the presence of my enemies;
You anoint my head with oil;
my cup runs over.
Psalm 23:5

*F*or what we are about to receive, the Lord make us truly thankful."

It's a familiar table grace—at least for those of us who still gather around the table at mealtimes and ask a blessing. We say it almost without thinking. It's just one of those standard mealtime prayers—easy to pronounce over a groaning holiday table when loved ones are gathered together.

But have you ever thought of praying that blessing for all the circumstances of your life? Have you ever thought of asking the Lord to give you the gift of gratitude for whatever life has poured into your cup?

That's what I'm trying to learn.

These days I am trying to pray this way on a daily basis.

"Lord, for *whatever* I am receiving and about to receive—pain as well as joy—please teach me the secret of giving thanks. For what I have already received— what has shaped my life in the past, and what is shaping me today—please fill my cup with thankfulness."

This is not an easy prayer to say with sincerity. In fact, I often feel a little hypocritical when I'm praying it. There are quite a few times in my life when I don't really *want* to be thankful.

I'm not particularly inclined to be thankful when there is upset and pain in our family. I don't really feel thankful for the chronic pain that some of my friends are suffering in their bodies. I'm certainly not up to offering a heartfelt thanksgiving when I feel like the world and even God have slapped me in the face.

Yes, I know we are supposed to "rejoice always, pray without ceasing, in everything give thanks" (1 Thessalonians 5:16-18). I believe that. But how often do the thank-yous come through gritted teeth? How often have I had to offer thanks because God said so, all the while feeling like a liar?

It's one thing to offer thanks because it's the right thing to do.

It's another thing to be truly thankful.

So how do I do it?

Only by remembering that all things come from God, including our own attitudes. An attitude of thankfulness is a gift God gives to us, a healing libation he pours into our cups. But we must choose to accept it, even to ask for it. Our part is to offer whatever is in our cup to the Lord, and then ask him to fill our cup with true thankfulness.

"For what I am about to receive, the Lord make me truly thankful."

What I am asking for, really, is an attitude adjustment. I am asking for a new way of looking at my life—past, present, and future.

Filling my cup with thankfulness for the past, for instance, means taking a step beyond forgiveness and opening my arms to the circumstances that made me what I am today. It means developing a new attitude toward the people and events that influenced me, even those who treated me ill or meant me harm. It means celebrating the good that God was able to do through those circumstances.

Yes, it's hard, especially for those of us whose childhoods were painful. For a few, filling our cup with gratitude for the past means just being grateful that it's over! But most of us who hold our cup of past pain up to the Lord will find that a thankful attitude can transform even painful memories.

I am finally reaching a place, for example, where I can honestly thank God for my father and even for the turmoil I experienced while growing up—not because that turmoil was part of God's plan, but because as I look back I can see God working in the midst of it all. As my attitude adjusts into a spirit of thanksgiving, I am able to see beautiful tracings of God's handiwork in my dark memories. For it was the turmoil and insecurity I knew in those days that made me so hungry to know a Father God, that gave me such a yearning for a Savior. Had my Jewish upbringing been happier or more secure, perhaps I would not have embraced the Messiah.

There are many other difficult areas of my past that I am learning to embrace, to see with eyes of gratitude. There may be painful things in your past, too, that need to be redeemed with the eyes of thanksgiving. Or perhaps there are hidden treasures, unappreciated legacies that begin to gleam when viewed in a thankful light.

I'm always amazed, for instance, when women complain to me that they "don't have a testimony" because they grew up in a Christian home. They seem sad or a little embarrassed that they don't have a dramatic story to tell of a radical life-change. It's as if they think they have somehow been robbed of the ability to have an influence for the Lord.

What a devious ploy of Satan—to turn a magnificent, gracious gift into a source of embarrassment! Being raised in a Christian home is a reason for profuse thanksgiving. Scripture, hymns, and Christian attitudes learned early become a fountain of enrichment for all of life. I have to really praise our grandchildren's parents for a good Christian foundation in their school and church. Tears fill my eyes when I see them praying or studying Scripture because I never had that kind of solid spiritual grounding in my young life. Whether or not God gives those children a dramatic "testimony," they will always have the Word of God deep in their hearts. That is good reason to be truly thankful.

But the attitude adjustment of thanksgiving is not just for the past. It's something I need every day in the present, and for the future.

To fill my present cup with thanksgiving means to live in the belief that God is working for good even when things seem to be falling apart.

And I find that harder to do right now than I have at any other time in my life.

The last few years have been difficult ones for our family. I have found it harder to trust God, harder to speak with confidence, harder sometimes even to get through the day. Harder, certainly, to live in thanksgiving. Day to day, my cup has been filled with pain.

And yet that is exactly why I so desperately need the attitude adjustment of thanksgiving. I need it to give meaning to my pain, to redeem it with the reminder of what God has to offer me in my hurtful circumstances.

And what does God give me in my pain? What reason do I have to be thankful?

First of all, he offers the gift of comfort—a significant mercy.

The promise is stark and direct in the King James version: "I will not leave you comfortless" (John 14:18). Other translations say it differently: "I will not leave you all alone" (TEV), "I will not leave you desolate" (RSV), "I will not leave you as orphans" (NIV). But the message is the same.

You may be hurting, says the Lord, but I will be with you all along the way. If you trust me, I will provide you comfort.

I have been comforted profoundly at times, in the very center of my pain, by a simple sense of God's presence, the nearness of the Holy Spirit. I can come to him and simply lean on him, drawing comfort from his nearness. Sometimes I pray, sharing my troubles and asking for his help. Or sometimes my knees buckle and I sink down wordless in the arms of my heavenly Father. If I pray on a disciplined, consistent basis, my prayer closet is likely the first place I want to go when my cup fills with pain.

And yet there are other times when I need the Lord's comfort in more concrete form. Especially during those times when my faith is weak or my spirit is overwhelmed or my body is failing me, I need God's presence to be incarnated—to take on flesh. And in those times he brings me comfort in the form of friends who love me and pray for me or simply watch and wait with me.

I will never forget the comfort a friend offered to me in Jesus' name during a time of awful physical pain. I learned later that I had picked up a parasite in my colon. But at the time I knew only that something was making my abdomen hurt. The pain quickly became so bad that I had to excuse myself from a dinner party and lie down. I lay there ten or fifteen minutes, curled up in a fetal position, fearful and hurting. And then my friend Susan came in. She put her arms around me and prayed for me, and I felt that God had sent an angel to comfort me. The pain didn't stop or go away, but it became tolerable. I was able to go home and sleep, and the next day I went to the doctor.

A special source of comfort in times of pain is the companionship of those who have been through the same ordeal. There is a sense of camaraderie and understanding in shared pain, and I believe God uses that fellowship to extend comfort to his children.

Several years ago I broke my foot. I quickly found that while many people were sympathetic, those who had been through the same experience could offer a special kind of comfort because they really understood what I was facing. And now, whenever I see someone with a cast, my empathy and compassion begin to flow. I can honestly say, "I know exactly how that feels, how that pain can shoot, how that foot burns." In the same way, I can resonate with the pain of those who have lost a parent or who have grown up in an alcoholic home. I can offer them a special brand of comfort because I *know*. I understand.

That doesn't mean, of course, that I can't offer comfort to someone who is going through something I haven't experienced. If I am willing, God can work through me to extend his comfort to anyone in pain, just as he works through others to comfort me. I can offer my presence, my words. I can bring a casserole or volunteer to help with chores. I can offer myself to the Lord as a human expression of his comfort. And I know that he works through such an offering, because I have been on the receiving end. I have been deeply comforted by men and women who showed me the Lord's comfort.

For the Christian there's probably not much else that comforts the soul more than God's Word. I find the psalms especially helpful. They are so honest and direct. They remind me that I am not alone in my pain, and they carry me through my pain to renewed faith. They help me adjust my attitude to one of thanksgiving.

But the most compelling source of comfort I find in Scripture is the reminder that my Lord is no stranger to pain. He chose to become human, to share our pain in order to move us beyond it. He knows what it is like to be rejected, to feel physical discomfort and spiritual desolation, to pray that the cup of pain would be taken away. He knows what agony is like, even what death is like.

But there is more than companionship here. I learn this, too, in the pages of holy Scripture.

My Lord is with me in my pain, but he also is greater than pain, greater than fear, greater even than death. He is with me in the midst of my suffering, but he will also carry me beyond it. If I continue holding up my cup to him, he will do more than fill it, he will also transform it.

This promise of transformation is the second gift our Lord has to offer in my pain. And this is not a consolation prize. This is not a paltry offering I get in return for giving up on earthly happiness. What God promises me in the midst of my pain is real life, real joy, incredible growth, unbelievable beauty.

This is what God has had in mind for me all along. This is what he is doing in the midst of all my circumstances. In the long run, this is "what I am about to receive." I'm going to be changed into something wonderful.

Because I love to collect beautiful teacups and saucers, I love a little parable someone shared with me years ago. I have taken this little tale by an unknown author and retold it in a way that speaks most deeply to me about my own pain and my own transformation.

The story begins in a little gift shop, a charming establishment crammed full of delightful discoveries. A man and a woman have gone there to find a special gift for their granddaughter's birthday. With excited oohs and ahs, they pick up dolls and books and figurines, intent on finding just the perfect piece.

Suddenly, glancing into the corner of an antique armoire, the grandmother spies a prize.

"Oh, honey, look!" she exclaims, taking him by the arm and pointing. Carefully he reaches over to pick up the delicate teacup in his big hand. A shaft of sunlight from the window shines through the translucent china, illuminating a delicate design.

"Oh, isn't it pretty?" the grandmother sighs.

He nods, "I don't know much about dishes, but I'd have to say that's the best-looking cup I've ever seen."

Together they gaze at the beautiful little cup, already imagining their granddaughter's face when she opens her special gift. And at that moment something remarkable happens. Something magic.

With a voice as clear and sweet as the painted nosegay on the saucer, that teacup begins to talk.

"I thank you for the compliment," the cup begins. "But you know, I haven't always been like this."

A little shaken at being addressed by a teacup, the grandfather places it back on the shelf and takes a step back. But his wife doesn't seem surprised at all. Instead, she asks with interest, "Whatever are you talking about?"

"Well," says the teacup, "I wasn't always beautiful. In fact, I started out as an ugly, soggy lump of clay. But one day a man with dirty, wet hands started slinging me around, pounding me on a worktable, knocking the breath out of me. I didn't like this procedure one little bit. It hurt, and it made me angry.

"Stop!" I cried.

"But the man with the wet hands simply said, 'Not yet!'

"Finally the pounding stopped, and I breathed a sigh of relief. I thought my ordeal was over. But it had just begun.

"The next thing I knew, I was being stuffed into a mold—packed in so tightly I couldn't see straight.

" 'Stop! Stop!' I cried until I was squeezed too tight to utter a sound. Parts of me oozed out of the mold, and he scraped these away.

"If I could have talked, I would have screamed.

"But the man seemed to know what I was thinking. He just looked down with a patient expression on his face and told me, 'Not yet.'

"Finally, the pressing and the scraping stopped. But the next experience was far worse. I was plunged into the dark, and then the temperature began to rise. The air grew hotter and hotter, until I was in agony. I still couldn't talk, but inside I was yelling, 'Get me out of here!'

"And strangely, through those thick furnace walls, I seemed to hear someone saying, 'Not yet.'

"Just when I was sure I was going to be completely incinerated, the oven began to cool. Eventually the man took me out of the furnace and released me from that confining mold. I relaxed. I even looked around and enjoyed my new form. I was firmer. I had shape. This was better.

"But then came the short lady in the smock. She pulled out tiny brushes and began to daub paint all over me. The fumes made me feel sick, and the brush tickled.

" 'I don't like that.' I cried. 'I've had enough. Please stop.'

" 'Not yet!' said the short lady with a smile.

"Finally she finished. She picked up her brushes and moved on. But just when I thought I was finally free, the first man picked me up again and put me back into that awful furnace. This time was worse than before because I wasn't protected by the mold.

"Again and again I screamed, 'Stop!'

"And each time the man answered through the door of the furnace, 'Not yet!'

"Finally the oven cooled once more, and the man came to open the door. By that time I was almost done in. I barely noticed when I was picked up and put down and packed in a box and jounced and jolted some more. When I finally came to, a pretty lady was picking me up out of my box and placing me on this shelf, next to this mirror.

"And when I looked at myself in the mirror, I was amazed. No longer was I ugly, soggy, and dirty. I was shining and clean. And I was beautiful—unbelievably beautiful. 'Could this be me?' I cried for joy.

"It was then," said the teacup, "that I realized there was a purpose in all that pain. You see, it took all that suffering to make me truly beautiful."

And we can be beautiful, too. That's what God wants for us regardless of the circumstances of our lives.

That doesn't mean that God sends us pain just to test us. I don't believe that God kills off loved ones and tortures innocent children with incurable diseases and turns our friends against us just so that he can teach us a lesson. The God of the New Testament is not a sadistic deity who delights in sending trials just to see if we humans will make it through. He doesn't have to. The human race and the forces of darkness are quite up to the challenge of causing enough pain and suffering and rejection to go around.

And yet our God, through his magnificent powers of redemption, has never lost the upper hand. Whatever ugliness we encounter, whatever suffering we undergo, whatever pain we stumble through, he has the power to redeem it, if we continue to hold up our cups to him.

We can take the pain of our past and the pain of our present and allow that pain to encase us for a lifetime if we want to. But that isn't what God wants us to do. God wants us to bring our cup of pain to him. He wants to comfort us, and he wants to transform us into something beautiful.

And for his loving presence yesterday and today and tomorrow, we can be truly and sincerely thankful.

Savoring God's Word . . .
A Taste of Thankfulness

Sing praise to the Lord,
You saints of His,
And give thanks at the remembrance of His holy name.
For His anger is but for a moment,
His favor is for life;
Weeping may endure for a night,
But joy comes in the morning. . . .
Hear, O Lord, and have mercy on me;
Lord, be my helper!
You have turned for me my mourning into dancing;
You have put off my sackcloth and clothed me with gladness,
To the end that my glory may sing praise to You and not
     be silent.
O Lord my God, I will give thanks to You forever.

                              Psalm 30:4,5,10-12

Those who sow in tears
Shall reap in joy.
He who continually goes forth weeping,
Bearing seed for sowing,
Shall doubtless come again with rejoicing,
Bringing his sheaves with him.

                              Psalm 126:5,6

We do not have a High Priest who cannot sympathize with our weaknesses, but was in all points tempted as we are, yet without sin. Let us therefore come boldly to the throne of grace, that we may obtain mercy and find grace to help in time of need.

Hebrews 4:15,16

In this you greatly rejoice, though now for a little while, if need be, you have been grieved by various trials, that the genuineness of your faith, being much more precious than gold that perishes, though it is tested by fire, may be found to praise, honor, and glory at the revelation of Jesus Christ, whom having not seen you love. Though now you do not see Him, yet believing you rejoice with joy inexplicable and full of glory, receiving the end of your faith—the salvation of your souls. . . . Therefore gird up the loins of your mind, be sober, and rest your hope fully upon the grace that is to be brought to you at the revelation of Jesus Christ.

1 Peter 1:6-9,13

Rejoice always, pray without ceasing, in everything give thanks; for this is the will of God in Christ Jesus for you.

1 Thessalonians 5:16-18

Fill my cup, Lord . . .

I surrender my cup to you,

that you may fill it with service

and the sweetness

of your presence.

8

A Cup of Service

Surely goodness and mercy
shall follow me all the days of my life;
and I will dwell in the
house of the Lord forever.
Psalm 23:6

It's such a simple, beautiful process.

I hold up my cup to my loving, giving heavenly Father.

He cleanses me of the old, the impure, the bitter—empties my cup and wipes it clean. Then he fills my cup with living water—fills it with quietness, with encouragement and forgiveness, with trust and communion and strength and thanksgiving.

His blessings flow. My cup overflows.

But there is a catch.

Or rather, there is a requirement.

The Lord's blessings flow freely, but receiving them in my life involves two important acts on my part.

First, I surrender.

Second, I serve.

Surrender is the very act of holding up my cup, handing my life over to him. My Lord Jesus supplies everything I need in my life, but he also demands everything. He asks for the whole of my life—my heart and my soul and my mind.

Sometimes it feels like a blessed relief, sometimes a painful sacrifice, often a mixture of the two. But it's never, ever a bad bargain.

I give him all I can of me.

He fills me with all I could ever want of him. And then he gives me back myself as well.

I've learned this dramatic lesson about submission over and over in my life, but two instances stand out in my memory.

The first surrender came when I gave my life to Christ. That was a big step for a Jewish teenager from a dysfunctional family. Most of my relatives thought I was crazy; they were sure I was making the biggest mistake of my life. Or perhaps they thought I was just converting so I could be with Bob. Several predicted we would never last.

But my surrender to the Lord Jesus Christ at the age of sixteen was real, and it changed everything. I came to Jesus with my whole heart, held out the cup of my life to him, and he filled it with himself. In the years that followed, he honored my submission by continuing to fill my cup with blessings. I grew. I learned. I made plenty of mistakes and felt my share of pain. But I never doubted my decision to submit my life to Jesus Christ, the Messiah.

Many years later came a second surrender that was both quieter and more earthshaking. It happened about the time that our daughter Jenny was leaving for college.

I remember the day so clearly. Jenny had been packing for days, and now she was actually loading her little Volkswagen convertible with everything she needed in her dorm room—her clothes and her cheerleading stool and her teddy bears and her plants and her pillows. I helped her make trip after trip from the house to the car. And all the while I was thinking, *Well, this is it. This is the day we've been waiting for.*

You see, Bob and I had planned our lives carefully. We had decided to have our children while we were young so that when we reached our forties our children would be out of the nest and we would have each other again. So I was very excited as I watched Jenny drive down the hill in her little blue bug. I followed her down the driveway waving and blowing kisses. I watched that little car disappear around the corner. And then I headed back to the house, thinking, *Wow, this is great. No more kids, no more running in and out. No more mess and loud music and food all over the place and worrying about where everybody is. Now I've finally got my life back.*

I walked into the front foyer and just stood there breathing in the peace and quiet. Everything looked just perfect. Every picture on every wall was straight and dusted. Every knick-knack was in place.

I walked down the hall to Jenny's room, half expecting it to be a mess from all her packing. But it was perfect; she had left everything in order. *Well, Mom,* I thought, *you've trained her really well.*

I stepped into Brad's room—he'd been away a few years. Everything was perfect there, too. All his trophies and memorabilia were lined up neatly on the shelves, and his bedspread was perfectly smooth. Without thinking I reached out to straighten a book on the shelf, but it didn't really need straightening.

I walked back down the hall, thinking again that everything looked just perfect. The house was so quiet that I could hear myself breathe.

At that time Bob owned a mobile home company. The business was struggling, so Bob was putting in a lot of extra hours. I knew he wouldn't be home until very late.

And now I found myself thinking, *You know, my children don't really need me anymore. They've got lives of their own now.*

And I thought, *My husband doesn't really need me because he's working late and he's putting all his time and energy into his business.*

And I looked around my shining, perfect kitchen and I thought, *My house doesn't even need me. I can whip it into shape in just fifteen minutes a day.*

All of a sudden the loneliness and the confusion hit me like a blow to the stomach. *Who am I now? What is there left for me to do?*

I went into the bedroom, where I usually had my prayer time. Everything looked perfect there, too, but I didn't notice. I didn't even get down on my knees like I usually did to pray. I just slumped down on the floor and cried, "God, I don't understand this. Why am I feeling so awful? This should be the most wonderful day of my life."

And it was that very day, down on that perfectly vacuumed floor, that I surrendered again.

I said, "God, you can do anything you want with me. I'm yours. I submit myself to you today."

I had no idea then what would happen. But God knew. He was already in the process of putting together the events that would launch my life in a direction that still astounds me.

You see, right about this time, I was reluctantly in the process of becoming an author. For several years I had been speaking to women's groups about home management, and my friend and mentor Florence Littauer had been after me to write a book. "I can't write," I had told her again and again. So finally her publisher had arranged to turn some of my speaking tapes into a book called *More Hours in My Day*. I received my first copies a few months after God and I had that session on my bedroom floor.

Meanwhile, Bob had finally decided to pull the plug on his struggling business. He sold the mobile home company and began looking for something else to do. But when I was invited to promote my book on a radio talk show in Los Angeles, Bob said he was free to drive me into town.

It was supposed to be a twenty-minute interview. Rich Buhler, the host, talked to us briefly beforehand and told us what to expect. "We'll talk about your book for ten minutes, and then we'll put you on the phone lines for ten minutes so you can answer questions for any people who may call in."

That sounded all right to me. I was too dazed at the idea of being an author to have any real opinions, anyway. So we began the interview, and suddenly the phones begin lighting up like crazy. I answered question after question, and the call-in lights were still blinking when my ten minutes were up. "I've never had this kind of response to a call-in show," Rich said. "Do you think you can stay a little bit longer?"

I looked at Bob, and he nodded. After all, we were in downtown Los Angeles at four o'clock in the afternoon, and who wants to get on a freeway in downtown Los Angeles at four o'clock in the afternoon? "We can stay," I told Rich.

That twenty-minute interview turned into a three-and-a-half hour marathon. And we got home to find the answering machine light blinking furiously and the answering machine tape completely used up. More than forty-five calls had come in—all in response to that radio interview.

The next day I was slated to speak at a mother-daughter tea. Bob told me, "Honey, I'm going to be home tomorrow, so I'll call all these people back." But he didn't. In fact, when I came home the following afternoon he was so hoarse he could barely talk.

"You wouldn't believe what's gone on today!" he croaked. "I couldn't even get started on returning the messages because the phone has been ringing all day."

"I have prayed with women on the phone," he said. "I've given them household hints. And Emilie, don't get excited, but I have just booked you to speak in thirty-eight churches!"

I couldn't even speak. I just stared at him. All this was beyond my comprehension.

"I'll carry your books for you when you speak," Bob went on. "And when the phone stops ringing, then I'll go out and get a regular job."

That was fifteen years ago. Bob is still carrying my books, and doing so much more. Between us, we have written almost two dozen books, and we have done seminars across the United States and Canada. We have met and served with some of the great Christian communicators of our day. We have been received into the hearts of thousands of dear Christian men and women.

And what truly overwhelms me about it all is that I never set out to do any of this. I never planned to write books or have a ministry. Neither did Bob.

What we did do was surrender. We held up our cups to the Lord and poured out our own agenda and asked him to fill our cups with what he wanted for us. He did. And the results still leave me openmouthed. I can't believe it's me doing all this. But it is. In a way, I feel like I'm more "me" than ever. My life is richer, more exciting. I know I'm where God wants me to be right now.

And that's what surrender can do.

But a second thing is required of me in this beautiful process of having my cup filled.

The stream of living water is supposed to keep on flowing. It's not supposed to stop with me. Blessings stagnate when they remain in my cup. I need to pass them on to others through service.

And what is service? Service is honoring the Lord by doing what he has told us to do. And what he has told us to do is to love him first and then to love others as much as we love ourselves.

That's why true service and surrender always go together.

In order to truly serve, I have to surrender my right to have my own way, my right to put my own comfort first. In return, I experience the joy of giving, of being a conduit of God's blessing. And this is truly a great joy.

Yet the cup of service can be an acquired taste, like rich espresso or caviar. For most of us humans, service doesn't come naturally. We like having our needs catered to. We like being taken care of. We like being served more than we like serving. And if we do serve others, we typically expect something in return. We scratch a back in hopes of having our own scratched. Or we offer good deeds in the hopes of improving our own reputation or just to make ourselves feel virtuous. Selfishness and power games come far more naturally to most of us than true, loving service.

And that again is why surrender has to come first. We develop a taste for service only as we develop a taste for Jesus—as we learn from him and know what it is like to have our cup filled with his blessings. We learn it from his example, and from the example of others who do his will. And we learn to serve others as we learn to serve him. It all goes together. It's hard to have one without the other.

The good news is that our motives don't have to be unmixed before we can begin the act of serving others. We don't even have to be living in perfect surrender to Jesus. (How many of us manage to live in perfect surrender all of the time anyway?)

The beauty of living in Christ is that he can use us in his service just as we are. He can redeem our blundering efforts—and his living water sparkles just as brightly when served in our cracked cups.

That said, how do we actually go about serving the Lord and serving others?

One way to serve is through vocation, through doing the work God calls you to do. This may be what you do for a living or what you do as a volunteer. But if you can't find any way to serve God and your fellow humans through the work that you do, you need to find another line of work!

Bob and I feel enormously blessed that we are able to make our living in direct ministry, speaking and writing about the Lord. Yet a job doesn't have to be inherently "Christian" to offer opportunities for Christian service. You can wait tables for the Lord, treating your customers with respect and kindness. You can paint houses for the Lord, conducting your business fairly and praying for the occupants of the houses you paint. And you can certainly raise children for the Lord, because everything you do and say will make an impression on those little ones.

Another way I serve Jesus and others is through prayer. We all need to be filling our cup daily with prayer for friends, for those in authority, for our churches and our families, and for our children— especially for our children, because the only assurance we have of access to our children's hearts is through prayer and the power of the Holy Spirit. We need to pray for wisdom, pray for understanding, pray that they will grow up loving and fearing the Lord.

Prayer can be a form of service in itself, but it also increases our capacity and desire to serve in other ways. When I am coming to the Lord regularly in prayer, I am usually growing in compassion, growing in understanding, growing in my willingness to serve.

This aspect of prayer has made a big impression on me during the past year. I have fervently prayed for someone I love, someone I felt was making a series of wrong decisions. And as I have prayed, I have been reminded that while my prayer changes a lot of things, it changes *me* most of all. I just knew that if I prayed hard enough, this person would eventually change her mind and do what I thought she should do. What has happened, instead, is that I have gradually been able to turn her over to God. Now, instead of praying that she will follow a certain path, I find myself praying that whatever path she takes will bring her closer to God.

In the meantime, as I have prayed, I have also drawn closer to my heavenly Father. Gently he has shown me ways that I can truly serve this precious person without pushing my own agenda on her. Gently he has led me toward caring for her more unselfishly.

And caring is yet another important form of service. I serve God and others when I notice their needs and act in ways that will help them.

More than once I have learned lessons in that kind of caring from our children and grandchildren. Our daughter Jenny, who worked as a waitress when she was younger, has fine-tuned those beautiful waitress skills of serving others and making them feel cared for. I love to watch her when she entertains, noticing the needs of her family and guests and deftly tending to them.

Our son Brad, too, moves me to admiration with his sensitive spirit and servant's heart. I remember especially the way he served my mother, his grandmother, when she was growing older. We were a busy, bustling, fast-moving family. Grandma Irene couldn't move very fast. And Brad was always the one who would wait for her, take her arm, help her out of the car, and walk slowly so she could keep up. He served her in a beautiful way, and as a result they developed a special relationship.

Our little grandson Chad gave us another eloquent lesson in caring a couple of years ago when our whole family took a vacation in Mexico. We were shopping in the little town near our resort, and Chad spotted a woman with a tiny baby sitting on the sidewalk, begging. We had told the children that people might ask them for money and that they might want to give a little. But we were surprised when Chad pulled a five-dollar bill out of his pocket and gave it to the woman.

"Wow, Chad," said his big sister, Christine. "You gave her all your spending money."

He shrugged. "She needed it more than I did," he told us nonchalantly.

And tears came to my eyes at this beautiful example of caring and service. Chad wasn't responding to guilt or pressure. He saw the woman's need, he cared, and he did what he could to help her. That's true service.

I serve God and others when I notice people's needs and care about them and respond to them. But there is yet another way to serve. It is obvious enough to sound silly, but it's a challenge for many people.

Simply put, I serve through serving!

That is, I serve by performing the kind of ordinary, menial tasks that meet needs but seldom bring recognition and glory. Service can be scrubbing a toilet, cooking a meal, taking an elderly neighbor to the grocery store. Any of these humble chores, when done in Jesus' name, can be a graceful dance of love. In fact, this kind of mundane chore seems to have a special power to communicate the Lord's love. Surely that is why Jesus singled out this kind of service— feeding the hungry, visiting the prisoners, ministering to the sick—and stressed, "Inasmuch as you did it to one of the least of these My brethren, you did it to Me."

I hope I'm learning to do that. I hope I'm learning to hold up my cup to my Lord in surrender and get it filled with his love, then pour the love out in service to those around me. I want to be a better servant to the people who read my books and come to my seminars, to the people I worship with at church, to the people I encounter at the supermarket. And I want to be a better servant to my own family—these people I love the most are sometimes the most difficult for me to serve.

Every Christmas, Bob and I invite my entire extended family over for a holiday dinner. And you have to understand that this is not a typical Norman Rockwell scene. Many people attend my seminars and read my books and just assume that my life is perfect—beautiful home, loving family, adorable kids, all clean and shining and organized. But let me tell you a little about the people who sit around my table at Christmas dinner.

We have a doctor and a dentist, the president of a large shoe company, an attorney, and several educators. We also have a bartender, a masseuse, and several who are unemployed. A few of us are homeless or near homeless. One is homosexual, another is HIV positive, yet another is involved with New Age practice. There is an ex-convict, more than one person with chemical dependencies (some recovering), several children who were drug babies. Some are married, some are single, several are divorced or separated. And all are gathered at the home of their Hebrew Christian sister/aunt/cousin Emilie, whom they are sure is totally weird!

These people are all family to me. God gave me these people to serve, and he wants to pour out his love on them through me. I don't know how well or how unselfishly I carry out this task. We don't have very much in common, and our time together sometimes feels awkward. But when they leave, they always say they had a great time. And I always fill a tote bag of food (turkey to make a sandwich, half a loaf of bread, my ten-bean soup). I feel I fed them and loved them like Jesus would, and that feeling fills my cup to overflowing.

Then there was the year I sat on a stool in the middle of our living room with all these people around me and read *The Story of Three Trees.* Three grandchildren, who were five, seven, and nine at the time, wrapped themselves in blankets and pillowcases and acted out the whole story of the tree that became the manger. This was not a carefully staged pageant. It was an impromptu, volunteer production, a gift of love. And that night when my wide assortment of family left, they all said, "This is the best Christmas we've ever had."

And that's how service works. When the Lord fills our cup, he fills it to be used. He intends for us to fill the cups of others the best way we know how.

And when we do, the sweetness of his love and peace flows from cup . . . to cup . . . to cup . . . to cup.

In his name.

Amen.

Savoring God's Word . . .
A Taste of Service

And now, Israel, what does the Lord your God require of you, but to fear the Lord your God, to walk in all His ways and to love Him, to serve the Lord your God with all your heart and with all your soul.

Deuteronomy 10:12

Then the King will say to those on His right hand, "Come, you blessed of My Father, inherit the kingdom prepared for you from the foundation of the world: for I was hungry and you gave Me food; I was thirsty and you gave Me drink; I was a stranger and you took Me in; I was naked and you clothed Me; I was sick and you visited Me; I was in prison and you came to Me." Then the righteous will answer Him, saying, "Lord, when did we see You hungry and feed You, or thirsty and give You drink? When did we see You a stranger and take You in, or naked and clothe You? Or when did we see You sick, or in prison, and come to You?" And the King will answer and say to them, "Assuredly, I say to you, inasmuch as you did it to one of the least of these My brethren, you did it to Me."

Matthew 25:34-40

Jesus . . . knowing that the Father had given all things into His hands, and that He had come from God and was going to God, rose from supper and laid aside His garments, took a towel and girded Himself. After that, He poured water into a basin and began to wash the disciples' feet, and to wipe them with the towel with which He was girded. Then He came to Simon Peter. And Peter said to Him, "Lord, are You washing my feet?" Jesus answered and said to him, "What I am doing you do not understand now, but you will know after this." . . . So when He had washed their feet, taken His garments, and sat down again, He said to them, "Do you know what I have done to you? You call Me Teacher and Lord, and you say well, for so I am. If I then, your Lord and Teacher, have washed your feet, you also ought to wash one another's feet. For I have given you an example, that you should do as I have done to you. Most assuredly, I say to you, a servant is not greater than his master; nor is he who is sent greater than he who sent him.

John 13:3-16

Walk in love, as Christ also has loved us and given Himself for us, an offering and a sacrifice to God.

Ephesians 5:2

Fill my cup, Lord . . .

I offer my cup of me,

that it may be filled

to overflowing

with you.

Fill My Cup, Lord . . .

I will dwell in the house
of the Lord forever.
Psalm 23:6

Fill my cup, Lord.
I hold it up to you with outstretched hands,
My heart parched and thirsty for your living water.

Fill my cup with your love, Lord.
Help me to feel your hands holding mine,
feel your arms around me,
feel your love empowering me.
Fill me with quietness and encouragement and trust.

Help me to live for you when trials, difficulties,
and storms hit me and those I love so deeply.
Help me not to give up when giving up seems easier.
Help me to trust you when I don't feel like
trusting anymore.

When I know pain, fill my cup with prayer.
Teach me the secrets of service and surrender.

Fill my cup, Lord. I lift it up to you.
Lift me up to do your will with love and sacrifice,
Never forgetting what you sacrificed for me—
Your Son.
    My Messiah.
        My Lord Jesus Christ.

Help me, Lord, to accept where I am now.
Help me to know I'm not stuck forever in my
        circumstances.
Help me remember that the windows do open
        and that fresh breezes do blow in
            and that living water forever flows
                and that those who ask receive.

I'm asking now, Lord.
I'm holding my cup in my hands,
And I'm asking you to fill it . . . with you.
Fill my cup with
        God the Father,
            God the Son,
                and God the Holy Spirit.

And when my cup springs a leak,
As earthen vessels are prone to do,
Then I'll just have to ask again,
Trusting in your love
To fill me again . . .
      and thanking you!
          Amen

Notes

1. Beth Wohlford, "No Compromise," from Sunday bulletin of Wlllowcreek Community Church, 27 August 1995 p. 5.

2. C.W. Christian, "My Faith Is Small," Moonlight and Stuff self-Published, 1990. Used by permission.

$\mathcal{T}$o obtain information about
Emilie Barnes' seminars, tapes,
and other helpful time-management
products, send a self-addressed,
stamped envelope to:

More Hours in My Day
2491 Crestview Drive
Newport Beach, California
92663

Other Books by
Emilie Barnes

ℐ❥ ℐ❥ ℐ❥

A Cup of Hope

A collection of personal stories that reflect on the recent challenges Emilie has faced, including health problems, broken relationships, and the healing process. You will be encouraged by the wonder of God's unfailing peace and loving presence that will fill your cup with hope.

The Spirit of Loveliness

Exploring the places of the heart where true femininity and creativity are born, this book contains Emilie's personal insights into spiritual beauty, along with hundreds of "lovely" ideas for personalizing your home.

15 Minutes of Peace with God

Find inspiration and revival with this collection of 15-minute-a-day devotions. You will savor each brief, meaningful chapter as Emilie shares her insight and God's Word to help you deepen your faith and fully experience God's presence.

Decorating Dreams on a Budget
(with Yoli Brogger)

Interior decorator Yoli Brogger and Emilie Barnes offer affordable ideas to make every home decorating project simple, fun, and worthwhile.

More Books by Emilie Barnes

🌿 🌿 🌿

101 Ways to Lift Your Spirits
The Twelve Teas of Christmas
The 15-Minute Organizer
15 Minutes Alone with God
Christmas Is Coming
Come to My Party!
Cooking Up Fun in the Kitchen
A Cup of God's Love
Emilie's Creative Home Organizer
Help Me Trust You, Lord
If Teacups Could Talk
An Invitation to Tea
Let's Have a Tea Party!
Let's Make Something Fun!
Little Book of Manners
Making My Room Special
Minute Meditations for Women
More Hours in My Day
My Best Friends and Me
Safe in the Father's Hands

Simply Organized
Survival for Busy Women
Time Began in a Garden
Timeless Treasures
Whispers of Prayer